Historic Tales

of

FORT BENTON

Historic Tales
of
FORT BENTON

KEN ROBISON

THE
History
PRESS

Published by The History Press
Charleston, SC
www.historypress.com

Front cover, top: *Steamy Night at Madame Dumont's*, painted by Andy Thomas, depicts the environment in Fort Benton, the world's innermost steamboat port, when the night turned violent in the volatile mix of alcohol, ladies and gambling outside Madame Dumont's Cosmopolitan in the Bloodiest Block in the West. *Courtesy of Andy Thomas. Front cover, bottom*: The steamboat *Helena* wooding at night. *Painting by artist J.E. Trott, in author's collection. Courtesy of Peter C. Trott. Back cover, bottom*: Gustav Sohon painted this scene depicting the first arrival of steamboats at the Fort Benton levee in 1860. *Lithograph by Bowen & Co. Author's collection. Back cover, in copy*: The logo for River & Plains Society, the nonprofit that manages Old Fort Benton, the Fort Benton Museums Complex and the Overholser Historical Research Center (OHRC). *OHRC.*

First published 2023

Manufactured in the United States

ISBN 9781467154871

Library of Congress Control Number: 2023934821

Notice: The information in this book is true and complete to the best of our knowledge. It is offered without guarantee on the part of the author or The History Press. The author and The History Press disclaim all liability in connection with the use of this book.

To Montana's Indigenous peoples, bold pioneers and our Canadian friends across the Medicine Line for our shared tales and heritage.

To Fort Bentonites—past, present and future—for presenting history with passion.

To Karin and Ian Deal for constant help and interest.

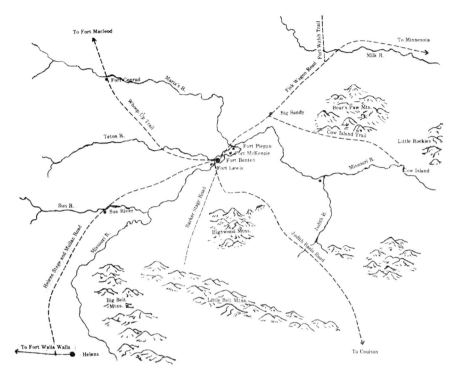

Trails radiated like spokes on a wagon wheel from Fort Benton, head of navigation on the Missouri River. *OHRC.*

CONTENTS

CONTENTS

INTRODUCTION

*H*istoric Tales of Fort Benton presents a dazzling sampling of the many dramatic events and colorful stories of the oldest continuously occupied outpost on the Upper Missouri River, deep in the heart of Blackfoot country. Trade opened on the Upper Missouri River in 1831 with Fort Piegan. A series of trading posts followed in the tense and rugged frontier environment as trade blossomed, treaties were negotiated and White settlement began amid varying degrees of culture clashes. With construction of the Mullan Road in 1860 and gold strikes and stampedes, an adjacent town of Fort Benton grew as the steamboat transportation hub and commercial center at the head of navigation of the Missouri River.

During the wild and woolly times of the post–Civil War 1860s, Fort Benton featured the "Bloodiest Block in the West," a "HooDoo Block" and vigilante justice led by famed lawman John X. Beidler. As both Indian agency and the world's innermost steamboat port, Fort Benton developed into a multicultural society and melting pot for White traders with Native wives and children, Black adventurers and Chinese merchants. The result was an astonishing mix of colorful characters and momentous events, with many tales to tell.[1]

Historic Tales of Fort Benton, through stories and photos, presents this dramatic environment as cultures merged and clashed, fortunes were made and lives were lost, amid a lively cast of heroes and villains.

A few notes are in order as the tales of Fort Benton flow forth. Many of the stories and words come directly from the colorful pioneer participants

American Fur Company Fort Benton Trading Post in August 1860. *Photo by Lieutenant James Hutton. OHRC.*

in this saga—you will be reading, unfiltered, many stories of Fort Benton, the Natives, the trading posts, the colorful characters and the frontier times. These pioneers speak the thoughts and words of their times—terms that may bother or offend today's reader: *savages, civilized, redskins, half-breed, squaws, papooses.* Let us understand their environment of forming a multicultural society with merging and clashing cultures and learn from these often tense, sometimes desperate times. Euro-Americans appear as "Whites," while Indigenous peoples are Native Americans or Indians. For centuries, French fur traders married Native women, with biracial offspring known as Métis, while the offspring of Blackfoot and other Indigenous women and American fur traders, known at the time as half-breeds, will be distinguished as *métis.* Since much of our story comes directly from those who lived in the times and "made" the history, remember this work reflects their stories in their terms—these are tales of their times, not repainted with today's terms.

The term "Old Fort Benton" is used today for the reconstructed American Fur Company Trading Post. In this book, "Fort Benton" is used, as it was at the time, for both the trading post and the adjacent town that grew in the early 1860s. These are tales of both the trading post and the town.

Through an act of ignorance, the first territorial legislature misspelled the county's name. "Choteau" County became one of Montana's nine original counties, and the name was not corrected to "Chouteau" until a legislative act in 1903. The original Choteau County extended from the Rockies eastward to the Little Rockies and from the Judith Basin to the unmarked Canadian border known as the "Medicine Line."[2] This massive area later comprised seven of today's counties besides Chouteau and parts

Fort Benton Trading Post blockhouse, built in 1846–47, with exterior logs replaced by adobe bricks in the 1850s. The blockhouse, the only structure remaining from the original trading post, was saved by T.C. Power money and Daughters of American Revolution (DAR) action in the early 1900s. This photo shows three ladies, trustees of Old Fort Benton, digging for beads: Antoinette Van Hook Browne of Fort Benton, Ella Lydia Arnold Renisch of Butte and Eliza A. Sturtevant Condon of Helena. *OHRC.*

of five others. Understanding the scope and size of the original county is essential to comprehend the problem of bringing law and order before railroads or automobiles.

The name Chouteau came from the family of St. Louis, prominent in the fur trade in the Upper Missouri region that became Montana. At the time, the sole White residents resided at Fort Benton, except for scattered missionaries, traders, woodhawks and a handful at the crossing of the Sun River on the Mullan Road.

Nor were residents in the least interested in payment of taxes or licenses to propel a far-removed territorial government, which by that time had migrated from Bannack to Virginia City. No representatives were present from Choteau County at initial sessions of the legislature or at a constitutional convention in April 1866. Worse yet, no taxes came in for the hard-pressed territorial government.

Two years after Montana Territory was created in 1864, a frustrated Governor Green Clay Smith lamented:

The county of Choteau has paid no taxes and the people refuse to organize or conform to the laws and perform their responsible duty....Officers have been appointed, but many of them and especially the commissioners refuse to act; hence there is no county government.[3]

Finally, on September 2, 1867, Choteau County residents organized a citizens' party and voted on a full slate of officers. These included the much-needed assessor, A.B. Hamilton, and county commissioners George Steell, George Baker and W.S. Stocking. Also, for the first time, citizens elected a sheriff, Asa Sample—after various earlier appointees. In the aftermath, the county assessed $438,887, but there were no apparent tax payments. Fort Benton residents did build a crude county jail, so apparently some local taxes were levied. For the year 1869–70, after the placer gold rush had played out, territorial taxes of $1,829.39 were paid. For two more years, members of the legislature's house were duly elected but didn't bother to make the long trip to Virginia City—they likely were busy trading north of the border in Whoop-Up Country. According to James Lowell, elected assessor in 1871, the previous assessor, Jeff Perkins, was a gambler and had depleted the treasury.

Throughout these years, Fort Benton was a melting pot bordering on a powder keg. Many of these men had seen Civil War service, both Yankees and Rebels, and not a few had killed before. Many had Native wives, and it was well into the 1870s before the presence of White women became common. The remoteness and minimal law and order attracted many southerners to their exile of choice on the Upper Missouri River, including many Confederate soldiers. Adventurous African Americans came, some working on steamboats, while others tried out their new freedom far from the failing Reconstruction of the South. They were joined by the Chinese who left the gold fields of southwestern Montana to operate restaurants, wash houses and opium dens. The Irish joined local southerners to keep Democrats in power politically throughout the new territory. Among the Irish in Fort Benton were an increasing number of Fenians, some coming directly from failed invasions of Canada and all bringing their hatred for all things British. Added to this mix, beginning in 1869, a depleted U.S. Army infantry company was stationed in the newly formed Fort Benton Military District to provide a semblance of security.

Montana's Indigenous tribes had grown increasingly dependent on trade and government annuities since the Lame Bull Treaty of 1855. These were the tribal lands of the Blackfoot Nation, the Niitsitapi or the Blackfoot

Confederacy, composed of the Kainai or Blood, Siksika or Blackfoot, Pikanii or Northern Peigan and Pikuni or Southern Piegan. The Southern Piegan "Blackfeet" lived in northern Montana, while the three "Blackfoot" tribes resided north of the Medicine Line in today's province of Alberta. The traditional lands of the Blackfoot Confederacy ranged widely from the North Saskatchewan River to the Yellowstone River and from Cypress Hills, east of the Sweet Grass Hills, to the Rocky Mountains.

In the words of William Gladstone, a visitor to Fort Benton from the British possessions up north:

> One could never tell when Sunday came around as there was no distinction made between that day and any other. Drinking and gambling and whiskey-selling went on just the same. On my first Sunday there I went to hunt up some friends and opening the door of the room where they lived, found four eager-eyed gamblers hard at work.
>
> Each man had a bag of gold dust and a pistol on the table before him. One of the men asked me if I was one of the parties that had just arrived from the north. I said, "Yes" and he asked me about the mines.
>
> "Stranger, do you indulge?" he hospitably asked and upon my admitting that now and again on rare occasions, I was known to do so, he pointed to a bucket and told me that I would find some knock-me-down in there.
>
> I dipped some of the liquid fire out of the bucket and asking for water was directed to another bucket which I found contained whiskey too. They all laughed at me and asked if they drank water where I came from as water in Benton was never used for that purpose.
>
> Oh, those were great days in Benton! Shooting and stabbing and rows of all kinds were daily occurrences, and it was a wonder to me that more men were not killed.[4]

From this intriguing environment, tales abound. This collection samples fourteen varied and lively tales, some famed but others largely hidden in the shadows of this complex multicultural society. You will meet gallant Lieutenant James H. Bradley, leading the 7th Infantry Mounted Detachment into battle during the 1876 Sioux War and riding to his death at the Battle of the Big Hole in the Nez Perce War, all while immersing himself in recording stories from the old fur traders in Fort Benton, leaving an amazing historical legacy. Among historian Bradley's many tales is the naming of the new trading post at a Christmas Eve ball in 1850. So much of what we know of the early years comes from Bradley's treasure trove.

The bold scheme to replace Fort Benton with Ophir, a new port downriver at the mouth of the Marias, fell victim to a Blackfoot raid with the massacre of ten woodchoppers in the spring of 1865. Shortly after, acting governor Thomas Francis Meagher's attempt to arrange a treaty with the Blackfoot featured an outrageous and near-disastrous scheme to fire a mountain howitzer from the back of an unsuspecting mule.

In an absence of law and order, fueled by the booming steamboat trade and the bountiful flow of gold, the Bloodiest Block in the West grew to a crescendo in post–Civil War Fort Benton. Never one to miss a gold camp boom or a lively transportation hub, Madame Eleanore Dumont moved her talent and girls into the Cosmopolitan, where she eased miners and pilgrims from their gold in the nicest sort of way.

As relations deteriorated and cultures clashed, no one worked harder than powerful Chief Little Dog to maintain peace, not only between Blackfoot and Whites but also between Native nations. He gave his life trying to keep the peace.

Distinctive characters left colorful tales, none more so than Irish revolutionary, Civil War hero and acting Montana territorial governor Thomas Francis Meagher. The mystery of his death in Fort Benton is surrounded by a mountain of legends and myths. Spend General Meagher's last day in Fort Benton with him and learn some intricacies of his legend. And, on her husband's death, join Mrs. Elizabeth Meagher, shrouded in mystery, on a trip through hell as she tries to reach her family home in New York, saving lives along the way.

While Montana's vigilantes in the gold camps were world famous, even the existence of Fort Benton's vigilantes has been hidden behind veils of secrecy over the years. Yet a vigilante movement was active in this lawless environment, and for the first time, much insight is provided about their activities, including their ties to the famed vigilante hangman John X. Beidler, who in later years became Fort Benton's de facto "marshal" as he ranged along the dangers of the HooDoo Block, into the saloons in the Bloodiest Block and down the rugged terrain of the Missouri River to bring the lawless to legal justice.

By the early 1870s, Fort Benton had become the focal point for trade and settlement north in the British possessions that became the Dominion of Canada. Fort Benton free traders moving into the lawless environment of the North West Territory forced the sudden formation of the North West Mounted Police. The Great March West of the new paramilitary police nearly ended in disaster, saved only by critical assistance from Fort

Blackfoot Confederacy Kainai students and elders from Alberta, Canada, led by Chief Roy Fox (*bottom center, in white hat*), visit the Overholser Historical Research Center to research their shared history. *Author's photo.*

Benton—leading to valuable trading relations and Fort Benton's role as the incubator for settling the Canadian prairie provinces of Alberta and Saskatchewan. Fort Benton's Overholser Historical Research Center, under the nonprofit River & Plains Society, today shares the historic tales of Fort Benton, Whoop-Up Country, our Indigenous peoples and our Canadian neighbors with all throughout the year.

With the eventual arrival of law and order on the Fort Benton frontier, the finest hotel in Montana Territory, the Grand Union, held the grandest of openings, highlighting the advancement of Fort Benton with the steamboat trade booming in the early 1880s. Arrival of the first electric lights on board the steamboat *Rose Bud* further demonstrated an evolution toward a refined and cultured town. It also highlighted the waning days of Fort Benton as a frontier settlement, a multicultural melting pot with an astonishing mix of Native wives with White traders, biracial marriages and métis children, African Americans and Chinese. Tentacles from this multicultural society extended to the survivors of the tragic Marias or Bear River Massacre of 1870 and to the exile years of the remarkable Louis Riel, a mystical blend of Mahatma Gandhi and John Brown, and his Métis and Cree followers. *Historic Tales of Fort Benton* brings the trading post, the town, the evolving eras and these colorful characters to life.

Chapter 1
THE BIRTHPLACE OF MONTANA

Fort Benton Commemorates 175 Years

Let us begin our tales with the grandest of all—a celebration held in Old Fort Park on June 25, 2022, to commemorate the 175th anniversary of the founding of Fort Benton. Join in the crowd at the park on that sunny summer afternoon as this author pays tribute to the Birthplace of Montana.

HAPPY 175TH BIRTHDAY, FORT Benton. We are the Birthplace of Montana—the oldest continuous non-Native settlement in Montana—a tiny St. Louis outpost on the Upper Missouri. And this is a special time and place—a moment in time we can commemorate together and a magical place at the head of navigation on America's greatest river, the Missouri River—from Lewis and Clark through the great steamboat era to the fascinating boat race from St. Louis to Fort Benton in 1937. The head of historic trails and rivers leading in every direction, like spokes on a wagon wheel—the bison trails, the Indian trails, the Mullan Road, the Whoop-Up Trail, the Fort Walsh Trail, the Northern Wagon Road, the Cow Island Trail.

Fort Benton was the incubator for our shared heritage with our Canadian neighbors in Alberta and Saskatchewan—from Fort Whoop-Up to Fort Macleod to ranches and settlement of the prairie provinces. The hub of our vast trading empire as Montana moved forward from territory to state—led by T.C. and John Power, I.G. Baker, the Conrads, Weatherwax and Wetzel and other merchant princes. The center for today's vast agricultural lands throughout the Golden Triangle—from open-range cattle and sheep ranching to the great homestead era that brought so many of our grandparents here.

If the walls of our historic blockhouse could only talk. What tales they could tell—tales of an ancient trading post rising from melted adobe mud into today's living history center Old Fort Benton, still growing and reconstructing. It's the tale of our Indigenous friends—Blackfoot, Gros Ventre, Assiniboine, Crow, Cree, Little Shell, Métis, from a welcoming Chief Little Dog to today's great Chief Earl Old Person. It's a tale of a small town with a big history—with steamboats arriving, giant Murphy wagons departing, the rough frontier streets from the Bloodiest Block and HooDoo Block to the tranquil, tree-lined streets of today: a multicultural society of colorful characters from its beginning.

It's a striking landscape, a land that belongs to God, captured dramatically by our painters—Karl Bodmer, John Mix Stanley, Gustav Sohon, Charlie Russell, Jim Trott, Dave Parchen, Brian Morger and others. It's a historical saga word-painted by our great historians: Lieutenant James Bradley, Johnny Healy, Joel Overholser, Hank Armstrong, Jack Lepley and others. It's the stories of our soldiers and sailors, men and women, off to wars abroad and at home, from Native warriors to frontier military to the great World Wars to Cold War proxies and on to the home front—serving our nation with duty, honor and country. It's the scene of masterful mysteries—from General Thomas Francis Meagher to vigilante justice to our dear, faithful dog, Shep. It's a tale of our pioneers, old and new, who knew they were facing danger down, making history and taking measures to preserve and present our unique history to the world.

Fort Benton's story begins with the great rivers, the Missouri, Sun, Marias and Teton, and the spectacular natural features from the five falls of the Missouri, along the White Cliffs on the Wild and Scenic River. The story extends to our Native Americans and the bison that roamed the land long before the arrival of American and British explorers, fur traders and settlers. Native Blackfoot long used the natural ford at Fort Benton, dubbed by them as "many houses to the South," to cross the Missouri River into the Judith and Musselshell hunting grounds on their seasonal rounds. Lewis and Clark made their fateful decision on the course of the Missouri at Decision Point, just around the bend downriver, and proceeded upriver past the Fort Benton bottom, on their way to portage around the great falls of the Missouri on their journey to the Pacific and destiny.

The story spans the fur and robe trade era, 1830 to 1870s, when Blackfoot and other Nations traded with St. Louis adventurers who moved up the Missouri to establish trading posts—first, 192 years ago at Fort Piegan at the mouth of the Marias River. A fateful visit to the successor trading post, Fort McKenzie, by Prince Maximilian of Wied and his artist Karl Bodmer captured both visual and word portraits of life on the Upper Missouri in 1833. In 1846–47, Alexander Culbertson built Fort Benton as a trading post for the Upper Missouri Outfit of Pierre Chouteau Jr. and Company.

In 1859, steamboats arrived a few miles downriver from Fort Benton delivering trade goods, Indian annuities and passengers and taking furs and bison robes down to eastern markets. As the head of navigation on the Missouri River, Fort Benton became the hub for the St. Louis to Fort Benton steamboat trade from 1859 to 1889, bringing many thousands of tons of freight and passengers to the frontier.

The summer of 1860 proved a transformational moment at the Fort Benton Trading Post. Three military groups arrived during July and August that year. First came Major George Blake and a regiment of dragoons by the

Blackfoot Confederation leaders, including Chief Earl Old Person (*center*), at Old Fort Benton in 2005 for the 150th anniversary of the Lame Bull Treaty. *Author's photo.*

steamboats *Chippewa* and *Key West*. Captain William F. Raynolds arrived two weeks later, coming down the Missouri River from its headwaters at Three Forks after exploring the Yellowstone Basin. On August 1, Lieutenant John Mullan with his expedition arrived at Fort Benton after blazing the 624-mile Mullan Military Wagon Road from Fort Walla Walla—the first interstate highway in the Northwest, connecting the Columbia and Missouri Rivers.

With gold strikes at Gold Creek and Bannack in 1862, Fort Benton became a major transportation hub. Fort Benton merchant princes formed trading and freighting empires extending from Fort Benton in every direction to the mines and camps throughout Montana and northward up the Whoop-Up and Fort Walsh Trails to Canada. Fort Benton supplied military posts at Fort Shaw in the Sun River Valley, Fort Assiniboine to our northeast and forts to the south. These were turbulent days, and the streets of Fort Benton were roamed by the rich and famous, angels and scoundrels, merchants and gamblers, Natives and soldiers, Irish Fenians and exiled Métis and by women and children with their welcomed warmth and taming influence.

During the height of the steamboat era, Fort Benton underwent a building boom with many brick buildings replacing original adobe and log cabins. The trading firms powered vast business empires that, in the words of historian Paul Sharp, made Fort Benton the "Chicago of the Plains." This was a time of made and lost fortunes and larger-than-life characters.

Railroads brought immense change as Fort Benton evolved to ranching, with tens of thousands of cattle and sheep on a thousand hills of the open range from the Judith Basin into the grasslands of Canada and large shipments to markets in Chicago. In the early 1900s, the fertile lands of North Central Montana opened to dryland farming, with thousands of homesteaders arriving by rail with their grain production shipping eastward. Fort Benton became the trading center for ranchers and farmers in the heart of Montana's Golden Triangle agricultural region.

Testimonials to Old Fort Benton have kept our old trading post on the national scene through the years. Over a century ago, the *Flathead Courier* paid tribute to the historic blockhouse at Old Fort Benton:

> *The strip of riverbank at Fort Benton…forms one of the most historic waterfronts in America, for along its length during the quarter of a century between 1860 and 1885 the beautiful river steamers from St. Louis unloaded yearly vast stores of merchandise for the Upper Missouri country and the gold camps of Montana, while millions upon millions of dollars in gold dust were taken aboard here for the trip down the river to the mints.*

Fort Benton in August 1868 with steamboat *Success* moored along the levee. By 1863, the town of Fort Benton had begun to grow upriver from the fort. Photo by C.R. Savage. *Author's collection.*

Along this strip of river frontage stepped ashore many of the pioneers who later became makers of Montana history, and it was here that the ill-fated General Thomas Francis Meagher fell from the deck of a steamer tied to the bank and was drowned one night.... The square tower near a grove of trees, far up the bank is the remaining bastion of old Fort Benton, most famous of the historic outposts of the northwestern frontier.[5]

Fort Benton's history forms around the tales, legends and people making their mark during each era of history. The Blackfoot and other tribal Nations, who historically made their seasonal rounds, were eventually confined to reservations. The early Chinese and Black Americans made their mark and then moved on, adventurers like traders Johnny Healy and Al Hamilton, fearless lawman X. Beidler, cowboy artist Charlie Russell and his cavalry friends from Fort Assinniboine, military leaders like Admiral Ulysses Grant Sharp and the legendary loyal dog Shep. Historic buildings rose, like the Grand Union Hotel, built at the height of the steamboat era in 1882, now restored to its elegant grandeur; the Choteau House, now Fort Benton's most endangered structure; the grand Chouteau County Court House, built in 1884 and still splendid today; the I.G. Baker home, undergoing preservation back to the way it was the day of that fateful last dinner for General Meagher

A rare photo of the North West Fur Company Trading Post taken in 1868 by Scout Charles Bucknum. *OHRC.*

in 1867; the Church of the Open Range, St. Paul's Episcopal Church; the Culbertson House, restored and going strong; and the Fort Benton Iron Bridge, the first bridge across the Missouri River in Montana, that began with a steamboat swing span and continues today as a scenic walking bridge.

Fort Benton became a National Historic Landmark in 1961 and then a Historic District on the National Register of Historic Places. Fort Benton is a Preserve America city, on the National Lewis and Clark Historic Trail and the river entry port for the 149-mile National Wild and Scenic River System and the Upper Missouri Breaks National Historic Landmark. In 2004, Fort Benton became a contributing site on the Nez Perce (Nee-Mee-Poo) National Historic Trail in recognition of Fort Benton military and civilian forces at the skirmishes of Cow Island and Cow Creek Canyon.

Fort Benton presents five exceptional museums. The Museum of the Northern Great Plains features Montana's State Agricultural Museum, the legendary Smithsonian Buffalo, a Homestead Village and a community events center. The Museum of the Upper Missouri presents "Twenty Tall Tales of the Upper Missouri," a sampling of Fort Benton's storied past. Old Fort Benton, a combination of the original blockhouse and reconstructed buildings, presents a living history fur and robe trading post with displays interpreting Blackfoot culture and fur trading days. The Starr Gallery of Western Art displays Bob Scriver's *No More Buffalo* bronzes interpreting Blackfoot life from "before the horse" until "after the buffalo" as well as Karl Bodmer's scenes of the Upper Missouri. Newest is the Upper Missouri Breaks Monument Interpretive Center, which features Chief Joseph's surrender rifle, a replica of the cabin of the famed steamboat *Far West* with its original bell and telegraph, a full-scale cut-out Murphy freight wagon and natural history features from the Upper Missouri. The Interpretive Center's distinctive exterior presents a scene reminding visitors of the White Cliffs of the Missouri.

Today, on this 175th anniversary, Fort Benton presents much of its historic character. The steamboat levee is now a park running the length of the community and featuring many interpretive signs. As you follow the levee along the walking trail from the Interpretive Center down to Old Fort Benton, you walk hallowed ground through the pages of sparkling history.

In the words of Montana poet Thomas Murray Spencer on an 1890s visit to Fort Benton:

> *Though its glory has departed.*
> *And its crumbling walls decay,*
> *History throws a halo round it*
> *That shall never fade away.*[6]

Chapter 2

MONTANA'S FIRST
GREAT HISTORIAN

Gallant Lieutenant James H. Bradley

Lieutenant James H. Bradley, a brave Civil War and Frontier War soldier, was Montana's finest early historian before his tragic death in 1877 at the Battle of the Big Hole during the Nez Perce War. This is his fascinating tale.

James Bradley was a man of many talents. Born in Ohio in 1844, at the outbreak of the Civil War in April 1861, he enlisted in the 14th Ohio Infantry Regiment at age sixteen. During his three months' service with the 14th, Private Bradley took part in actions at Philippi, Laurel Hill and Carrick's Ford, Virginia. Mustered out in August 1861, he entered Oberlin College but could not sit out the war, so he enlisted in Company F, 45th Ohio Infantry, in June 1862 to serve through the war's duration. Bradley was promoted to full corporal on January 14, 1863, and was captured in a skirmish near Philadelphia, Tennessee, in October 1863. Imprisoned at infamous Andersonville, Georgia, for six months, he survived that ordeal to be released through a prisoner exchange. Corporal Bradley rejoined his regiment and fought in the battles of Kennesaw Mountain, Peach Tree Creek, Jonesboro and the siege of Atlanta. He was promoted to full sergeant in February 1865 and mustered out on June 12, 1865, at Camp Harker, Tennessee.

Commissioned second lieutenant in the 18th U.S. Infantry in April 1866, Bradley's first duty post was Fort Phil Kearny in the Powder River country, protecting the Bozeman Trail, the new route to the Montana gold fields. After promotion to first lieutenant in August 1867, Bradley transferred

Lieutenant James Bradley, Fort Benton's first great historian, collected stories from early traders at Fort Benton in the early 1870s before he was killed in action at the Battle of the Big Hole during the Nez Perce War. *Author's collection.*

with the 18th Infantry to Reconstruction duty in Atlanta, Georgia, where he met and married Mary Beach.[7]

In April 1872, Lieutenant Bradley and his Company B, 7th Infantry, arrived at Fort Benton Military Post. There, Lieutenant Bradley handled his military duties with ease and often served as post commander. He had an insatiable curiosity and focused his interests on science and history. As he talked to the many old-timers from the fur trade era in Fort Benton, he assembled their stories as a labor of love and with the skill of an experienced historian. In the span of just three years, Lieutenant Bradley recorded a remarkable collection of diaries, journals and letters from his historical research, forming more than eleven volumes of historical writings. He was the right man in the right place, and his monumental contribution to Montana history presented unique information on the early history of Fort Benton, the fur trade of the Missouri and Yellowstone valleys and the Indian tribes of the region.

Bradley's years in Fort Benton spanned a critical stage in the evolution of the head of navigation on the Missouri River as it emerged from the fur trade era and evolved from a raucous to a more mature frontier mercantile town. At this time, White women and children began arriving in Fort Benton, among them his wife, Mrs. Lieutenant Mary Beach Bradley. The great fur traders of the Upper Missouri—Alexander Culbertson, James Kipp and many others—still lived around Fort Benton. Pioneer merchants like T.C. Power, I.G. Baker, W.G. and Charlie Conrad and others found Lieutenant Bradley an inquiring and thorough chronicler of their experiences and anecdotes. The many encounters between Native Americans and newly arriving miners and settlers of the past decade were still fresh in the memory of the town's old-timers as well as many métis and Native participants.

Company B remained at Fort Benton until September 1, 1875, when they were rotated to Fort Shaw. With Montana's most violent Frontier Wars breaking out, tension and separation filled life at the Queen of Montana's military posts. On March 17, 1876, a battalion of the 7th Infantry known as the Montana Column, with Company B and Lieutenant Bradley commanding the mounted detachment, left Fort Shaw for Fort Ellis to join the Yellowstone Expedition against the Lakota Sioux Indians. In one of the ironies of this campaign, at the very time Custer's men were being overwhelmed, the Montana Column could find very little action. Lieutenant Bradley's mounted troops were first to discover the dead of Custer's command on the Little Big Horn. Bradley chronicled this campaign in a journal that proved his skill as an observer, historian and writer. His journal, first published in 1896 in volume 2 of the *Contributions to the Historical Society of Montana*, later came out as *The March of the Montana Column: A Prelude to the Custer Disaster*. The Montana Column returned to Fort Shaw on October 6 and remained in garrison over the winter.[8]

In late July 1877, Colonel Gibbons and most of the 7th Infantry—including Lieutenant Bradley, leading his mounted infantry—departed Fort Shaw to intercept the Nez Perce in western Montana. On August 9, at the Battle of the Big Hole, Lieutenant Bradley was killed in action leading an assault by his Mounted Detachment on the Nez Perce camp. One of his men called to him just as he was entering a thicket where Nez Perces were believed to be waiting: "Hold on, lieutenant; don't go in there; it's sure death." But he pressed on, regardless of his own safety, and just as he reached the edge of the brush, an Indian rose up within a few feet of him and fired, killing Lieutenant Bradley instantly. The Nez Perce was immediately riddled with bullets, and then the men charged madly into the brush, dealing death to every Nez Perce who came in their way.[9]

A model officer, a brave soldier and Montana's first great historian was dead. The *Helena Herald* paid tribute to the gallant Lieutenant Bradley:

> With great sorrow we chronicle the death of this brilliant young officer. In the fierce battle of the Big Hole, fought with the Nez Perces on the morning of August 9th, his body lay first among the slain.
>
> James H. Bradley was First Lieutenant, Company B, Seventh Infantry Regiment, part of Col. Gibbon's depleted force of less than one hundred men marching from Fort Shaw viz Cadotte's pass, to Missoula. Thence on with the column, increased by the platoon of men under Browning, marching from Ft. Ellis, and Rawn's and Logan's skeleton companies from the post at Missoula, in hurried pursuit of the hostiles to the Big Hole, where death overtook him in the thick of the fight and at the head of his men.
>
> Lieutenant Bradley was not alone known and appreciated as a tried-and-true soldier. He excelled in literary culture, and his sprightly and

The 7th Infantry at the Battle of the Big Hole, by R.F. Zogbaum. Harper's Weekly, *December 28, 1895.*

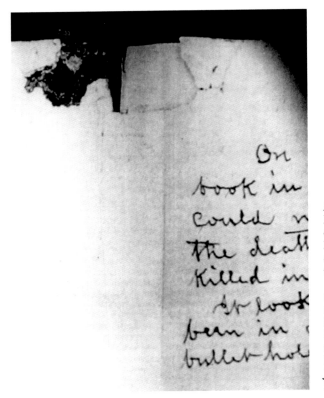

Left: A bullet, likely at the Battle of the Big Hole, damaged the cover of Lieutenant Bradley's copy of the *Contributions of MHS*, volume 1. *Author's photo.*

Opposite: Lively masthead of the *Benton Record*, the first newspaper in northern Montana Territory that carried writings by Lieutenant Bradley and John J. Healy. *Benton Record, June 16, 1876.*

entertaining pen made his name familiar to thousands of our people. His prose and poetry at intervals for several years brightened the columns of the local press, the HERALD *especially having been favored in this respect. Other and broader themes shared his attention as well, and manuscripts of solid worth, applying to the earlier voyageur occupation of the Northwest, are valuable mementoes left of his untiring, thorough, and enthusiastic historical research. His thrilling description of the Custer Battle Field, published in the* HERALD *and telegraphed to the country, is still fresh in the memory of our readers. He commanded Gibbon's Crow Scouts throughout the Yellowstone campaign of 1876 and was the first man to reach the scene of the frightful massacre and bore back to the approaching column the news of the terrible disaster.*

Riding among the slaughtered cavalrymen he found the body of the fearless Custer, and about him within the space of five rods square, forty-two of his slain men. The whole tragic scene was faithfully depicted in the Lieutenant's own graphic language and coming from the first eyewitness

VOLUME II.—No. 5.
WHOLE N., 80. | Fort Benton, M. T., June 16, 1876. | $3.00 PER ANNUM,
POSTAGE PREPAID

of the battlefield following the massacre, it went forth on lightning wings to 40,000,000 people. In this hour of sorrow, sympathy will strongly express itself for the suddenly bereaved wife [Mary Beach Bradley] *and fatherless little one* [May]. *Our people will recall the young bride of a few years ago journeying with her husband from the far South to Montana. Arriving at Helena, the husband, falling sick with a dangerous malady, lay near death's door. The infection of the pest house carried with it the terrors of death, yet the young wife was his constant nurse, nor could she be coaxed or driven from his bed side. She could die, she said, but she would not in life separate from him who was her husband, her all. We console the widow; we mingle our tears with hers and invoke consolation to her wounded heart in this her sorest hour of trial.*[10]

After Lieutenant Bradley's death, Mary Bradley and her daughter, May, boarded the steamboat *Benton* and departed Fort Benton on August 17 bound for St. Louis, en route to Mary's family home in Atlanta. Mary Bradley was pregnant at the time of her husband's death, and her daughter Pauline was born in Atlanta not long after her arrival there. Through the efforts of 7th Infantry commander Colonel John Gibbon, Mary Bradley graciously presented her husband's exceptionally valuable manuscripts and historical research to the Montana Historical Society; thus, Bradley's history remained in Montana.

The life of gallant Lieutenant James H. Bradley, young Civil War soldier, survivor of Andersonville, Indian Wars leader and Montana's greatest early historian, was cut tragically short. Ironically, at the very time that Lieutenant Bradley's life was ending, the *Helena Herald*, the *Benton Record* and other territorial newspapers were publishing many of his historical articles. Scholars today still recognize Bradley's historical material as literary gold.[11]

NAMING THE UPPER MISSOURI TRADING POST: FORT BENTON

A Plea for Fort Benton
By Cavalier[12]

In the year of our Lord 1850, a joyous party assembled on Christmas evening in a recently constructed adobe building at the trading post of the American Fur Company, on the Upper Missouri River, known as Fort Lewis. In the gathering there was a two-fold objective: to celebrate the advent of Christmas by suitable rejoicings, and to dedicate to its ultimate uses the first adobe building erected within the present limits of the Territory of Montana. Major Culbertson—then in the prime of life—was there as chief of the establishment and gathered around him were his sixty or seventy white subordinates, who constituted the garrison of the fort, with their wives and children; and the reader needs only to be told that the great majority of the former were Canadian and Louisiana French, of the class called voyageur, to know that merriment and jollity reigned supreme. Several violins were in active operation, and to the flow of sweet sounds, scores of nimble feet tripped merrily, and joyous voices mingled in the bursts of jovial song.

At last, during this rousing carnival, the tall form of Major Culbertson was seen to rise and signal silence. When the uproar had subsided sufficiently to permit his voice to be heard, he addressed the assembly in a little speech, in which he recounted the noble qualities of one of America's distinguished sons [Senator Thomas Hart Benton]; *dwelt particularly upon his services a few years before in behalf of the American Fur Company, when he rescued it from a ruinous litigation that threatened the complete overthrow; and proposed that in his honor the post, then in process of construction in adobe, should from that time forward be known as Fort Benton. With loud cheers his audience signified their approbation, the violins struck up a lively air, and dancing was renewed with increased vigor, and passing from lip to lip of the hilarious assembly, the name of Fort Benton went forth to the world, and is now recorded in millions of maps from one end of civilization to the other.*

This was the first christening of the embryo city at the head of Missouri River navigation, and so well was it done that it was reasonable to expect that no other would be deemed necessary. But, presto, change! No more do

Left: Alexander Culbertson, founder of Fort Benton Trading Post, as painted by John Mix Stanley in 1856. Displayed at the Dean & Donna Strand Gallery, Fort Benton. *Author's photo.*

Below: Alexander Culbertson and Natoyist-Siksina, aka Natawista, his Kainai wife. Bronzes by Marlene Hankins Nielsen. *Author's photo.*

we see Fort Benton a remote, isolated trading post in a broad wilderness wholly possessed by the red savage. Gold has been found in Montana, thousands of stalwart men gather in her gulches, and the vast supplies thus rendered necessary find their way to the mines mainly through the Missouri River. A new and extensive business is created at Fort Benton, and under the walls of the old fort a town begins to spring up; and presently comes a band of surveyors, who trail their chains awhile in the river valley, and then, by a silly trick of words, call the few scattered buildings, and the many vacant squares they have laid out, "Benton City."

Ye gods! What an outrage was this! What an insult to the old fort that for years had looked down grimly upon the ground thus desecrated, sole lord of it all! How could propriety stop short of preserving the sonorous old name, the centre of so much interesting history, in this new-born village—this city, if you will, but still desperately cramped in the confining limits of its swaddling clothes?

This was the second christening, but the good sense of its population caused it to meet with little favor. The town is still known as Fort Benton, the post-office is Fort Benton, freight is still consigned to Fort Benton, and when sometimes cut short in the pronunciation by its inhabitants it is always done as an abbreviation, with the whole symmetrical name in the background of the speaker's mind. But now we come to the consideration of the most formidable attack upon the old name that it has yet received. We now boast a newspaper [Benton Record], *and it is a creditable production. It is pleasant to reflect that our town now has a worthy champion against all future "adverse journalism." Can this paper, this champion, this advocate of our interests, be a robber in disguise that would deprive us of aught valuable? It would seem so, for it is not despoiling us of our good name, even in the sense we use it, one of the first of measures. We find by the paper itself that it is the Benton RECORD, published in Benton, M.T., and every time it alludes to our town it is as Benton—not once as Fort Benton.*

Oh, Mr. Editor and proprietor of the RECORD, would that you had looked into Lippincott's Gazetteer of Geography before you did this thing! Let me tell your readers what you would have found there. You would have found that, within the limits of the United States, there are already fifty-two geographical localities in possession of the name of Benton, where there is but one called Fort Benton, and that is our town. And now you have despoiled us of all the advantages of our singleness of possession and humbled us ruthlessly into such a nest of Bentons that it is bewildering to try to identify ourselves.

Thus, have we been three times named, and there is no guarantee that we have reached the end of it yet. Permit my indulgence in a little speculation as to where the thing seems tending. Fort Benton, Benton City, Benton, Bentown, Buntown, Bunghole! That sounds ridiculous but truly, it is scarcely in advance of what has already happened. But let us halt here and retrace our steps. Let us go back to the first and best name of them all, and forever hold fast to it. Benton is truly a good name, but it violates our early traditions, and there are in all conscience, enough Bentons in the country already. Fort Benton is a better name, it is in keeping with our traditions, it perpetuates our fur-trading and military history, and it is a name that really makes us a peculiar people, since the world over we have no participants in its possession.[13]

Chapter 3

THE DEATH OF A BOLD SCHEME

The Ophir Massacre

*F*rank Moore, captain of the steamboat *Cutter*, organized a group joined by Nathan W. Burris promoting a bold plan to supplant Fort Benton as the head of navigation of the Missouri River. In the spring of 1865, they launched construction of the town of Ophir at the mouth of Marias River, downriver thirty miles from Fort Benton. The Ophir Plan was just the tip of the iceberg for the grandiose scheme of the promoters. Suddenly, on May 25, 1865, ten woodcutters from the new town's construction crew were murdered by a party of Kainai led by Chief Calf Shirt. The ten men and the bold scheme for Ophir crashed and died that day in May 1865.

THE TRAGIC NEWS TRAVELED TO THE MINING CAMPS

News traveled by horseback in the pre-telegraph days of territorial Montana. The "melancholy" news of the Ophir Massacre arrived at Virginia City in time for publication in the June 3 *Montana Post*. Written the day after the massacre, it warned:

> *Fort Benton, May 26ᵗʰ, 1865.*
> *TO FREIGHTERS AND TRAVELERS:*
>   *Indians have killed, at Ophir, ten men, among whom are N.W. Burris, Frank Angevine, John Andrews, and Abraham Lott. Parties travelling to this place should go in large parties and well-armed.*

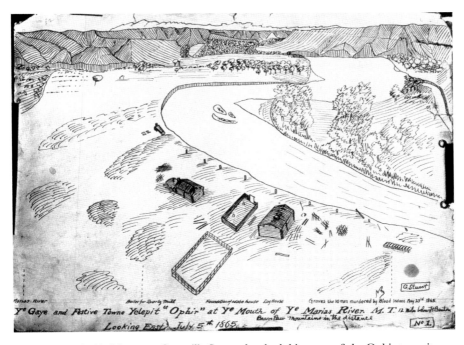

Just after the Ophir Massacre, Granville Stuart sketched this scene of the Ophir townsite near the mouth of the Marias River. *OHRC.*

MILTON & TAYLOR,
F. M. THOMPSON,
THOS. DORRIS,
CARROLL & STEELL.[14]

GOING TO THE MOUNTAINS

In the spring of 1864, businessmen of St. Paul organized the Idaho Steam Packet Company, under Captain Abe Hutchinson, to send two steamboats, *Cutter* and *Chippewa Falls*, to the Upper Missouri. On April 18, the two steamers departed La Crosse, Wisconsin, for their long trip down the Mississippi River to St. Louis and up the Missouri to the new gold camps then in Idaho Territory. Heavily loaded with passengers and freight, they proceeded to Fort Randall, Dakota Territory, where on May 19, General Alfred Sully impressed the *Chippewa Falls*, captained by Hutchinson, to carry supplies and ferry troops for a military expedition against the Lakota Sioux. Its passengers and freight were transferred to the *Cutter*, under Captain Frank Moore, to proceed on to Fort Benton.

Chippewa Falls loaded army supplies and proceeded to Fort Union and then up the Yellowstone River, supporting Sully's expedition. *Chippewa Falls* proceeded about fifty miles up the Yellowstone, becoming the first steamboat to navigate that river. After returning to Fort Union, it loaded sixty-five thousand army rations and, accompanied by the *Alone*, proceeded ninety miles up the Yellowstone River in support of the army. *Chippewa Falls* was not released from service until October 23.[15]

The steamer *Cutter*, a small sternwheeler built for the Upper Mississippi trade, proceeded with its heavy load slowly up the Missouri River. By July 14, *Cutter* had reached the mouth of the Marias River and, encountering engine problems, could not continue to Fort Benton. The 250 passengers and 200 tons of cargo were off-loaded and taken by freight wagons to Fort Benton, while Captain Moore attempted to repair the engines. He planned to load passengers and freight for a late-season trip down the Missouri in September.[16]

WINTERING AT THE MOUTH OF THE MARIAS

The engine problems persisted, and Captain Moore concluded it best to winter his boat at the mouth of the Marias, having there a safe eddy for protection against ice gorges. *Cutter* passed the winter without sustaining any damage while awaiting new engines to be shipped upriver in the spring of 1865. Captain Moore understood the strategic location that surrounded him—this was the site where Lewis and Clark, in the spring of 1805, camped for an extended period while trying to decide which river was the true Missouri River.

This, too, was the site where James Kipp constructed Fort Piegan in 1831, the first trading post on the Upper Missouri. And this was the locale where the Blackfoot nations often camped along the Teton and Marias Rivers when preparing to receive treaty annuity goods and trade bison robes and furs with the trading posts at Fort Benton, the American Fur Company post and its opposition post, Fort Campbell. With the beginning of the town of Fort Benton outside the trading posts just as the Civil War ended and steamboat traffic dramatically increased, saloons and alcohol became readily available, and incidents of violence increased. Since the

Blackfeet Agency was located at Fort Benton, annuities were dispensed there, and trade operated at both trading posts, yet the tribes sought to distance their camps from the growing town.

Looking around, Captain Moore saw the area as the perfect site for a city. It could capture some of the shipping traffic, extend the shipping season longer and perhaps even supplant Fort Benton as the head of navigation on the Missouri River. He drew up plans for a town of Ophir on the south side of the Marias; a North Ophir, where the town of Loma is today; and an East Ophir, across the Missouri, to prevent a rival town from springing to life there. All three prospective towns would be 320 acres in size.[17]

THE BIRTH OF A BOLD PLAN

Captain Moore was a born speculator and promoter. Seizing on his situation, he began to cultivate friendships and soon became a favorite with men of influence in the new Montana Territory. Throughout the winter, the cabin of the *Cutter* was the scene of numerous parties during the long evenings as the captain raised money, sold lots and worked on charters for the essential wharves, warehouses, freighting roads and even prospects for a future railroad. In addition, Captain Moore rode over the surrounding country, examining the Missouri River carefully between the Marias and Fort Benton, and concluded that Benton was too high up to serve as the head of navigation, requiring steamers to pass difficult shoals and rapids above the mouth of the Marias.

The captain traveled to Virginia City in company with Nathan Burris, a town promoter and builder from Iowa, and Bob Dole, son of Commissioner Bob Dole of Indiana. They returned to Fort Benton via the Missouri River above the Falls, taking soundings along the river to determine the possibilities of navigating the upper river with specially built steamboats. The five Falls were also examined, and at various favorable points, locations were marked out for manufacturing towns and future cities.

The first session of the Montana legislature convened at Bannack in the winter of 1864–65, and when Moore and his comrades returned to the capital, they with their allies were granted a charter for the exclusive right to navigate the Upper Missouri for a term of twenty years and to establish the towns of Ophir, East Ophir and North Ophir, embracing both sides of the Marias River for some distance above its mouth and on the bottomlands of the Missouri opposite these points.

It isn't clear whether Captain Moore's company ever intended to place steamboats on the river above the Falls, but they were serious regarding the new towns, as they proceeded at once to gather a crew of hardy adventurers to assist in building Ophir. The company, with Burris in charge, began construction in the spring of 1865, setting up a sawmill, warehouses, cabins and corrals. Everything proceeded smoothly until the evening of May 25, when Burris, with nine men, a team of oxen and a wagon, left to go west up the Marias about five miles to float three hundred previously cut cabin logs downstream to the site.[18]

The Tale of the Ophir Massacre

There are many versions of the cause and account of the Ophir Massacre. Among the most credible are those provided by Abe Hutchinson, clerk of the steamboat *Yellowstone*; Captain Joseph LaBarge of the steamboat *Effie Deans*; Sheriff Neil Howie of Virginia City; and adventurer John J. Healy. The following composite tale from these sources seems most plausible, beginning with Johnny Healy.[19]

Steamboat *Cutter* and the Ophir Massacre

The Siksika and Kainai Indians of the northern Blackfoot were being encouraged in their hostility toward Montana Territory's White settlers by the traders of the Hudson's Bay Company, who hoped to maintain their monopoly of the Indian trade by provoking bad feelings between the northern Indians and the Whites south of the Medicine Line.[20] Native and White cultures clashed as young Natives conducted horse raids that led to increasing incidents. Despite strong efforts by Chief Little Dog and other leaders of the southern Pikuni Blackfeet to maintain peaceful relations with White settlers, by 1865, incidents had increased virtually to a stage of open warfare.

Greatly complicating the situation was the fact that the Fort Benton Trading Post was transitioning to new ownership by the North West Fur Company and that the town of Fort Benton was rapidly building in the bottomland adjacent to and just upriver from the fort. Further problems came from the location of the Blackfeet Indian Agency, which was in the town. Thus, Blackfoot had to come to Fort Benton to conduct much of their trading of bison robes and furs for consumer trade goods. In addition, the tribes received their Indian annuities at the agency. This complex situation would remain until 1869, when at last the agency was moved seventy miles west of Fort Benton to a site near today's town of Choteau, along the Rocky Mountain Front.

Into this powder keg, a noted warrior of the Kainai Nation approached Fort Benton with two other Kainai, taking pains to show contempt for several White men who were scattered around the fort. The Kainai were not molested for a while, and gaining courage from the apparent timidity of their enemies, they now began to count coup against the Whites, recounting their deeds of bloodshed and plunder. Among Plains Indians, counting coup was the warrior tradition of winning prestige in battle by showing bravery in the face of an enemy and intimidating him, thus persuading him to admit defeat without having to kill him.

This sealed their fate. Henry S. Bostwick and Joseph Spearson waited until they finished their tales of blood and then shot all three, throwing the bodies into the Missouri River.[21]

This affair occurred early in May, and the news was swiftly carried to the Kainai camp along the Sun River, causing wild commotion among the tribe. The chiefs of the Fish Eaters, Fat Horse and Black Elk bands marshaled about two hundred men, led by their respective chiefs, Calf Shirt, Medicine Sun, Un-es-tina and Big Snake, and proceeded toward Benton via the Goose Bill, arriving at the Marias River on the morning of May 25.

Meanwhile, the projected town of Ophir had progressed so far that ten men were sent out to float timber down the Marias for the first buildings. Just above the mouth of the Teton, the men were surprised and alarmed to discover a formidable force of Indians riding down upon them. Unfortunately for them, instead of retreating to a more favorable point of defense or attempting to fortify themselves in any way, they opened fire at once without waiting to find out the Indians' intentions.

John J. Healy, years later, was told by some of these same Kainai that no harm whatever was intended for the woodcutters. The Kainai claimed that they were going to Benton to learn why the Whites had killed members of their tribe and to either fight or make peace, according to the result of their inquiries. When they were fired on by the woodchoppers, they were astonished and called on them to stop, and the chiefs endeavored to restrain their warriors from returning the fire. The White men were likely ignorant of the meaning of their gestures and cries or were too frightened to understand either. They continued to fire on the Indians until the latter charged them, and they were taken down by overwhelming numbers. Healy recounted:

> *I could never get any of the Indians to acknowledge how many of their own number were killed. They said all the men stood their ground and fought like lions except one who was well mounted and attempted to get away. He was followed and his horse stumbling, left him at the mercy of the foe. This was Burris. He was killed where his horse fell with him, and being a light, delicate man, his resistance must have been of short duration. There were two brothers, named Friend* [Franklin and George W. Friend], *and a colored man* [James Berry] *in the party, who it is said took up their positions behind two trees, and fought like tigers until surrounded and shot down.*

SHERIFF HOWIE'S ACCOUNT

Shortly after the massacre, Sheriff Neil Howie arrived at Fort Benton with an initial deployment of territorial militia intended for service against the Indians. Receiving the news, Sheriff Howie rode on to Ophir with a four-man scouting party—Captain Frank Moore, Colonel John H. Rogers, Captain Nick Wall and Malcolm Clarke—and on to the scene of the massacre. While there, Sheriff Howie and his party visited a nearby camp of Pikuni Blackfeet.

Sheriff Howie and his party went to the scene of the massacre with a man named Woods, who had been up and had taken a view of the bodies of the slain and of the locality. The trail from the steamboat *Cutter* crossed the Teton, which the party forded; they then proceeded up the Marias about a mile and a half from the steamer. Sheriff Howie described the scene.[22]

> *The river bottom between the Marias and the bluffs was about four hundred yards wide. Close to the river the brush was rather dense, but more scattered towards the middle of the bottom, where the ten men were killed. There were two large cottonwood trees, about 75 yards apart. At the foot of one of them, Andrews was killed and "fearfully mutilated." Burris was found about fifty yards below his horse, which was half a mile nearer the boat than the bodies of the other murdered men.*
>
> *The rest were scattered from thirty to a hundred yards from each other. The circumstances appeared to preclude the idea of a surprise. They must*

Site of the Ophir Massacre about 1930, several miles up the Marias River. *OHRC.*

Old cottonwood tree at the site of the Ophir Massacre. *Author's photo.*

have seen the Indian camp, for no man would turn a wagon where they did, in the narrows, having a fine open spot a little ahead. Probably the Indians discovered the whites about as soon as the whites saw the Indians, and while they were getting their ponies, the party started back for the boat, and were overtaken and massacred.

They did not expect the men at so late an hour. Very possibly, Burris was galloping home and was overtaken and shot from his horse, which being a lazy animal, the Indians killed, thinking it worthless.

The firing commenced with a regular volley and was rapid and continuous for fifteen minutes. The head chief of the band and another were killed on the spot, a third Indian was wounded, and is not likely recover. This statement was made by the South Piegans.

The noise of the skirmish was distinctly heard at the Cutter; but though thirty men were there, who well understood what was going on, no one stirred. Two or three signified their willingness to go, but none went. Captain Moore was absent down the river.

The cattle were all shot together in the yoke, except one which was found the next day standing, badly wounded.

IN THE AFTERMATH

On the morning of the 26th, a party of men from the Cutter started with a wagon to find the dead men and bring them in—all ten bodies were found, brought to camp, and buried in one grave, side-by-side; with a stake placed at the head of each, with the name. N.W. Burris was formerly of Iowa; the names of the others, were: George W. Friend, Franklin Friend, Abraham Lotts, Henry Lyons, Henry Martin, Frank Angevine, John Alley, John Andrews, and James Pirie, [sic, Berry] (colored).[23]

According to Sheriff Howie, the Pikuni Blackfeet were very scared. They had sent a deputation to Benton; but were afraid to come in, and therefore camped on the Teton. When the sheriff, Capt. Moore, Col. Rogers, Capt. Wall, and Malcolm Clarke went out to the camp, the Pikuni brought out about thirty head of stolen horses and delivered them over. They showed a fresh Kainai scalp, and said they were at war with that nation, and that if the Whites would only come in a large party, they would provide horses for them, and join in the attack on the Kainai.

The Pikuni said they knew that they could not fight the Whites; that they were too numerous, and that if they could, they were not disposed to

Top: Overlooking Ophir townsite from Lewis and Clark's Decision Point. *Author's photo.*

Bottom: Sign featuring Ophir, the Town That Never Was. *Author's photo.*

do so, but that they were willing to fight the Kainai, with the Whites. The Kainai had told the Pikuni that they supposed the Whites would come after them, and that they were ready for them; that they were going to the Belly River, across the Medicine Line more than two hundred miles from Fort Benton. After the conference, a Pikuni deputation went to Benton with Sheriff Howie's party, and after doing some trading at the trading post, retired the next day.

Howie was convinced, from all he could learn, that the Kainai planned to return after they got their families to a place of safety, and commence war. There were a few Kainai in the Pikuni camp, and they said they had killed twelve Whites, and would kill more. Sheriff Howie's scouting party were very kindly treated and supported by merchants Carroll and Steell, and the other citizens of Fort Benton.[24]

THE DEATH OF OPHIR

The Ophir town enterprise perished at this time, and no effort was ever made to revive it. Captain Moore returned to the States with the *Cutter* and a large load of passengers that same spring and never returned to Montana Territory.

The killing of this party near the mouth of the Marias River inaugurated a new order of things. The Montana militia was at once organized and called out, which had the effect of keeping the Indians in check for a short while, but raids and incidents recommenced soon after.

THE INDIAN WAR

Captain Nick Wall, who had the complex job of coordinating arriving steamboat freight and moving it from Fort Benton by Diamond R freight wagons, demanded action, sending the following communication to his assistant, W.F. Bartlit, in Virginia City.

STEAMER DEER LODGE, *May 30, 1865.*

W.F. Bartlit: The Yellowstone arrived here on the evening of the 28th, at 8 P.M.; the Deer Lodge *this evening at 4 P.M. You have probably heard of the slaughter of ten men by the Indians. This is correct. The Indians are desperate and daring, and there is but little safety here. They are stealing horses, and mean war. There are various rumors and reports, all bad enough. I have just learned by your letter by Mr. Atchison that myself and party were killed. It is a mistake. I went some three hundred miles down the river, met the* Yellowstone *and came up on her. Carroll and Steele wrote to Gov. Edgerton, giving him an account of the depredations by the Indians, which is correct. See the Governor and call his attention to the matter. The time for him to act has come. I am satisfied the Blood Indians are bent on war, and I am fully convinced they will do much mischief if not checked. The Pagans and Blackfeet say they will not join the Bloods. I do not know whether they can be trusted or not. The Governor should raise three hundred and fifty or five hundred mounted-men and send them immediately. The Crows and Gros Ventres would be glad to have a hand in it.*

Send the messenger back as soon as you can, with letters and information of what is to be done. Something must *be done. No person can go out of sight of the Fort with safety. Truly, yours,*

N. WALL[25]

Chapter 4

THRILLING SCENES

The 1865 Fort Benton Treaty Council

illiam T. Hamilton—or "Uncle Bill," as he was fondly known—left the last of his many stories with anthropologist George Bird Grinnell. Uncle Bill's wide knowledge of Montana's history was based on his own half century of adventures. His last story was of the great treaty council of the northern plains Indians at Fort Benton in 1865 just months after the Ophir Massacre.[26]

This treaty council—like so many others, called for the purpose of robbing the Native Americans of their hunting grounds—was, in Hamilton's view, a farcical and highly dangerous undertaking. The result yielded no understanding that was observed, but it did result in a huge gathering of some five thousand Blackfoot Confederacy and Atsina (Gros Ventre) on the Fort Benton River bottom. In Hamilton's assessment, this was a gathering of powerful tribes that were hostile to each other, resulting in a narrow escape from a massive battle that threatened to wipe out the small White population living around Fort Benton.

Indian Agency clerk Hiram D. Upham arrived on the steamboat *Twilight* at the end of July and described the small town that he found:

> *Above the fort stands the imposing collection of houses, designated by the inhabitants thereof as "Benton City."…We shall have six streets here as soon as we get 5 more. The city consists of 12 to 15 log houses. These are used as dwellings, stores, warehouses, and saloons. When the [wagon] trains are in here things are very lively indeed. The drivers then all get*

drunk and as they all carry a revolver and knife and as fights are a daily occurrence, it makes everything look lively.

Four men have been shot since I have been here. As there are but few laws in force here, and no officers at all to execute them, these chaps have it pretty much their own way.

The office of the Indian agency stands in about the center the city. Over this department at present, I reign supreme. The mansion itself is built of logs, and the large crevices between the logs are stopped up with mud. The roof is made by laying down slabs and covering them over with about 6 inches of dirt....

The chief productions of Fort Benton are Frenchmen, half breed Indians, buffalo robes and dogs. The surrounding country abounds in buffalo, deer, antelope, elk, mountain sheep, rattlesnakes, mountain lions, grizzly bear, and hostile Indians.[27]

Bill Hamilton's vivid description of one of the most picturesque events in Montana history, the 1865 treaty, and the part he played in it, flows from his story:

From 1863 to 1865 a chronic state of warfare existed between all the Indian tribes of Montana territory. During this warfare, miners and freighters had sustained serious losses in stock, and many miners and settlers had been killed by the Indians....

In 1864 "Uncle Bill" Hamilton left the White settlement at Hellgate, near Missoula today, and went to Fort Benton, where he built a log hotel and proceeded to operate it. He was appointed sheriff of Choteau County [in 1866] by Governor Green Clay Smith, and at the same time was appointed deputy United States marshal. At that time Choteau County was as big as the state of New York.

The population at Fort Benton was a motley one. There were some trappers and free traders, mostly good men. The remainder were employes of the Fur company, in all about 45 White men. There were also some halfbreeds, the outstanding one of which was Joe Kipp, a good friend of Hamilton. The North West Fur Company had bought out the old American Fur Company....Carroll & Steell, former clerks of the old fur company, had opened a store at Fort Benton....

The territorial delegate at Washington [Samuel McLean] had asked for protection for the white inhabitants against the Indians, and a commission of three persons was appointed to consider this matter. It

Fort Benton scene as it appeared in an 1868 photo by scout Charles Bucknum. *OHRC.*

consisted of Acting Governor Thomas Francis Meagher, Judge Lyman H. Munson and E.W. Carpenter. They arrived at Fort Benton early in September 1865, and determined that the [Blackfoot Confederacy], *Gros Ventre* [Atsina], *and Crow* [Apsáalooke] *Indians must be brought into Fort Benton and there induced to make a permanent peace.*

Runners were sent out to invite the [Blackfoot Confederacy], *to come in, but no one could be found who would undertake to hunt up and bring in the Crows and Gros Ventres. The reason was that the country between the Missouri river and the Yellowstone was overrun by war parties of Sioux, Cheyenne, Arapahoe, and Blackfeet. A war party considered all who did not belong to their own party as enemies and acted accordingly.*

HAMILTON'S SERVICES ENLISTED

The commissioners sent for Bill Hamilton and urged him to carry the message to the Crows and Gros Ventres, which tribes were hunting somewhere in the country infested by war parties, and after some persuasion, gained his consent. He was considered the only white man available who could perform this service.

Hamilton informed the commissioners that he must have a certain Piegan Indian, named Eagle Eye, for a companion on the trip. A runner was sent to

Little Dog, head chief of the Piegans, and in two days Eagle Eye reached Fort Benton. Hamilton had once saved his life. He was a cool and brave Indian and would die for Bill if called upon to do so. He had accompanied Hamilton on two previous trips of great danger.

Hamilton selected his two fastest horses for himself and secured two almost equally good saddle animals for Eagle Eye. They took along an extra pack horse, carrying presents for the Gros Ventres and Crows. Hamilton was armed with the first Henry rifle that ever came into the territory; a repeating weapon that cost him $106. Eagle Eye had a Sharp's rifle. Each carried a brace of .45 pistols. Eagle Eye also carried his bow and arrows.

Eagle Eye, on the way to Fort Benton, had met a war party of Piegans, who told him that the Crows had been camped at Medicine Springs between the North and South Moccasins, but had moved their camp. Hamilton also learned from his companion that there were three Blackfeet war parties out after Crows and Gros Ventres.

"Locate Crows and Gros Ventres"

The route taken by Hamilton and Eagle Eye took them across Arrow Creek, 30 miles from Fort Benton; thence to Rattling Buttes at the east end of the Highwoods, where Eagle Eye killed a buffalo cow with his bow and arrows to avoid rifle fire, which might attract war parties. From there a trail to Wolf Creek, near where Stanford stands today, was taken, where the trail of a Blackfeet war party was struck. The two messengers followed across Willow creek and reached the Judith River, and finally, after some exciting experiences, reached Medicine Springs, between the Moccasin ranges, where they found the Crow village had been encamped.

They followed the travois trails across an open and dangerous country to the east end of the Judith mountains and went from there to Flat Willow creek.... They pushed on to the Musselshell, finding many traces of Indian war parties, and from the forks of that stream toward the Bull mountains.

Heading for Porcupine creek, where they expected to find the Crow, they were attacked by a party of five Blackfeet Indians. They let them get within 60 yards; then showed themselves and ducked. The Indians foolishly fired their flintlock guns, and before they could reload or draw their bows, Hamilton and Eagle Eye killed the five Blackfeet. Eagle Eye was afterward blamed by the Piegans for killing the Blackfeet, but he felt entirely justified in doing so under the circumstances.

SIOUX AND CROWS BATTLE

When the Crow camp was finally reached, Hamilton and Eagle Eye found a battle raging, the camp having been attacked by a war party of Sioux numbering 200. The Crow warriors totaled 300. Hamilton joined the Crows in the fight, and the Sioux were soon routed, leaving several slain on the prairie. These the Crow scalped.

Hamilton then gave some presents to the Crows and told them his errand. The head chief of the Crows said they could not go to Fort Benton, as their ponies' feet were tender and there was little game between where they were and the Fort. They said, further, that they had been told to go to Fort Union, at the mouth of the Yellowstone, the next moon to meet some white chiefs in council.

Hamilton and Eagle Eye then made a beeline for the mouth of the Musselshell River and forded that stream. They then struck out for the Little Rockies, near where they met the Gros Ventres, who agreed to push on toward Fort Benton.

By the time Hamilton and Eagle Eye reached Fort Benton the [Blackfoot] began to come from the north. Three days after their return a steamer from St. Louis arrived with a large load of presents for the Indians attending the council. By then the total number of Indians camped on Fort Benton bottom was upward of 4,000, and another thousand arrived.... The Indians from the north pitched their lodges mostly on the upper end of the bottom, while the Gros Ventres placed their camp some three hundred yards east of the old Fort, at the lower end. Formerly the Gros Ventres and the Piegans and Bloods had been friends, but for the past four years they had been at war and there was bitter hatred between the tribes. Hence this wide separation of their camps.

The council chamber at the Blackfeet agency had been put in order, with the American flag handsomely displayed. The Gros Ventres chiefs at first refused to attend the council through fear of their numerous enemies, but on promise of protection, they came in.

THE FORT BENTON TREATY

September 20, 1865, the reading of the treaty began. This was a formidable document of some 50 closely written pages. The clerk began reading it by sections, which then had to be interpreted, first by the

This 1865 building, one of the town's first, served as the council house, the Blackfeet agency and, later, as Sullivan Saddlery, pictured here. Joe Sullivan poses beside his shop. *OHRC.*

Today, this historic council house and saddlery is part of Charles and Sue Ford Bovey's collection at Nevada City. *Author's photo.*

interpreter for the [Blackfoot]*…and then by the interpreter for the Gros Ventres. Hamilton at once saw that it would take weeks to get through the documents at that rate. So did Little Dog, the Piegan chief, who told his interpreter to inform the council* [that they needed to condense the] *verbose legal phrases, to a wild, restless lot of Indians, 90 per cent of whom had no desire to mix with or deal with the whites, except to trade for certain commodities of which they stood in need. The commissioners were entirely at sea about the matter, but Hamilton and the interpreter effected a condensation of the treaty in simple language that could be read and translated in a very brief period.*

The following morning the council met again. The Small Robe band of Piegans claimed all the land on the south side of the Missouri river as far south as the Musselshell. They ceded in the treaty all their rights to this territory. Other Piegan and Blood Indians claimed land along the summit of the Rockies south to the Little Blackfoot River, and thence southeast to the Missouri river. In the treaty they ceded all the territory from the mouth of the Marias River up to the Marias to the Teton river, following the middle of that stream to its source, for a stipulated sum to be given to them for 20 years. The Gros Ventres had no land to cede. Neither did the [Canadian] *Blackfoot, and according to the views of many the latter had no right to be present at the treaty.…Some of them wore medals given by the English sovereign.*

INDIANS GET UGLY

All the country east of the Teton river was set aside for a Piegan and Blood reserve, and Hamilton states with much truth that, without the influence of some of the mountain men who were present and were friends of the Indian chiefs, the treaty could not have been made at that time. Undoubtedly Hamilton's influence was invaluable, although he believed the Indians were being done a great wrong. He saw, however, that [they] had no alternative than to submit, and that fighting would only make things worse for them.

The next day began the distribution of the presents, which lasted two days and was replete with funny incidents. The commissioners then left for Helena with the Indian agent at Fort Benton, Gad E. Upson. Hamilton declared that the latter knew as much about an Indian as he [Hamilton] knew about the inhabitants of Jupiter.

The commissioners had hardly disappeared up the trail for Helena than Little Dog, chief of the Piegans, came to Hamilton and told him that the North Piegans, Bloods and the Blackfoot had secured some whisky and were getting ugly and singing their war songs. Little Dog advised the whites to remain in their houses. He believed that the three bands he mentioned would attack the Gros Ventres camp and might also try to wipe out the whites.

Hamilton and some of the other whites loaded a 12-pound brass cannon and placed it at a point of vantage. Rifle pits were dug and there were 45 whites to defend them. At the Fort the North West Fur Company's men, numbering 12, locked themselves in and prepared for a siege.

AN EXCITING SCENE

Hamilton, with Little Dog, who was a firm friend to the whites and a fine Indian, and Eagle Eye, then rode to the Gros Ventres camp. The Gros Ventres had already been warned and had pitched their lodges in a circle, their ponies corralled, and rifle pits dug all around the village. All the warriors were stripped to the breechclout and painted. Little Dog informed them that he would try to prevent the hostiles from attacking them and advised them not to shoot first if the hostiles came. He declared that he and his people would be their friends, meaning, by his people, the South Piegans. Hamilton then rode to Little Dog's camp with him, where they found the young warriors preparing for battle.

At this time, much bad blood existed between the North and South Piegans. Hamilton visited all the camps and told the chiefs that they must control their young men.

About 11 o'clock in the morning 500 naked warriors in war regalia, painted and mounted on their best ponies which were also painted, rode down the bottom toward the Gros Ventres village, yelling and uttering their war-cries. The ground trembled under the thundering hoofs of the ponies. Everyone expected that a fight was on and wondered where it would stop. Little Dog had 60 warriors at the upper end of town. Hamilton remained with him. The Indians rode furiously around the Gros Ventres camp. If one shot had been fired by either party a bloody fight would have followed, as the Indians who were held back by their chiefs would then have joined their friends. Hamilton said that if a fight had started Little Dog would have joined the whites. He notified the hostile bands that if they attacked the whites, they would have him to fight. The advice he gave the Gros Ventres about not firing the first shot undoubtedly prevented the touching of the match to the powder.

The hostiles rode around the hostile camp many times, yelling, calling names, and challenging the Gros Ventres warriors to come out and fight; but the Gros Ventres remained quiet in their rifle pits, despite the hot blood of their young men. Finally, the mounted warriors rode back to their camps, stopping on the way near the agency building to sing war songs and to call the white men "dogs" and "women." The whites warned the hostiles to stop their talk, or they would kill them, and presently the riders gave a yell of defiance and left.

As the whites were eating a hasty lunch, a fearful yell was heard. Hamilton and Little Dog mounted their horses. Hamilton decided that if the hostiles attacked the town and Little Dog attacked the hostiles, he would remain with him. If Little Dog failed to act, he could return to the town and fight there.

The yell was given by 1,200 painted [warriors], each of them had tied from five to 20 yards of calico to [their] horse's tail, and they started out to run all over the bottom. Each Indian was trying to make his pony *step on the calico tied to the horse ahead. They were yelling and shooting in every direction. It was a wild orgy that would take the brush of a [Charles M.] Russell to paint.*

That night the Gros Ventres silently moved their village, without being discovered by their enemies. The next morning all the Indians except Little Dog's band left for the north. Before they left, two war parties of Piegans and Blackfoot had been organized to raid the miners and ranchers in the western end of the territory. Such was the result of the treaty. Most of the Indians were dissatisfied and looked on the whites with hatred. A chronic state of warfare between the tribes and between Indians and whites continued for years, as it had in the past.[28]

THE MULE AND THE MOUNTAIN HOWITZER: AND A WILD RESULT

Missing from Hamilton's account of the 1865 Fort Benton Treaty Council is a delightful tale, later presented in the *River Press*:

A large freight train of the Diamond R transportation company was also camped on the flats. They had transported a four-pound mountain howitzer on the back of a faithful mule from a steamer.... The howitzer had been left for the protection of the freight, which, on account of the extremely low stage of water, could not be brought to the fort by boat. With the last load of freight came the gun.

The immense congregation of Indians caused the men in charge of the "little gun" to conceive the idea of showing them its strength by discharging it from the back of a mule.... The howitzer, loaded with grapeshot, was securely fastened upon the back of a large, sleepy looking train mule with the muzzle pointed toward the tail. The patient, unsuspecting mule was led to the bank of the river near the site of the [later] T.C. Power & Bro.'s store, and a target set up across the river. The rear of the mule was turned toward the target and arranged in a semi-circle around the mule were the train men, officers, and wondering Indians, well besprinkled by our curious old-timers.

A chief of ceremonies having been appointed, he advanced, and when all was in readiness, inserted a time fuse in the touchhole of the howitzer, and then retired. In a short time, the quiet, unruffled mule heard a fizzing just back of his ears, which made him uneasy, and he immediately began

A Hot Time in Fort Benton, painted by Andy Thomas, depicts a true incident in Fort Benton in 1865 when a four-pound mountain howitzer strapped to the back of a mule was fired with surprising results while Native Americans looked on in amazement. *Courtesy of Andy Thomas.*

to turn his head to investigate. As he did so his body turned and the howitzer began to take in other points of the compass. The mule became more excited as his curiosity became more and more intense, and in a few seconds he either had his four feet in a bunch, making more revolutions a minute than the bystanders cared to count, with the howitzer threatening destruction to everybody within a radius of a quarter of a mile, or he suddenly would try standing on his head with his heels and howitzer at a remarkable angle in the air. The chief of ceremonies was so excited he was seen vainly trying to climb the flag staff; the train men and Indians scattered pell-mell over the flat toward the bluffs, running as if they thought in flight lay their only safety, and that, too, at a rate of speed much greater than grapeshot. Judging from the alacrity with which Col. Broadwater, H.A. Kennerly, and Mose Solomon slid over the bank of the river, they were not opposed to immersion; Matt Carroll, George Steell and James Arnoux sprinted toward the store, which occupied the present site of Sullivan's saddlery shop [the Council House]; *Hi. Upham, John J. Healy and Bill Hamilton began to throw up breastworks with their sheath knives, Capt. Nelse* [Vielleaux] *rolled promiscuously on the ground and groaned, while I.G. Baker and one or two of the peace commissioners were turning back-springs toward the fort.*

Left: Adventurous Indian trader and sheriff Johnny Healy wrote many historical articles during the 1870s. This author compiled Healy's stories in *Life and Death on the Upper Missouri: The Frontier Sketches of Johnny Healy*. *Author's collection.*

Below: This sheet-iron weather vane shaped in the silhouette of a bison withstood many years atop the kitchen's cupola at Fort Benton Trading Post. Legend has it that the damage resulted from the ill-fated firing of a mountain howitzer during 1865 treaty festivities. It is jointly owned by Montana Historical Society and River & Plains Society. *OHRC.*

River and Plains Society - Overholser Historical Research Center - Fort Benton - Montana

While the mule, with his heels in mid-air, was shaken with the most violent agitation, there was a puff of smoke, a thud, and the mule— oh, where was he? Ask of the winds, for not a soul saw him, and they will tell you a lonely, forlorn mule might have been seen turning over and over until he tumbled over the bank with his howitzer and cast anchor in the river, while the shot went toward the fort, striking the figure of a buffalo [weathervane] that was used as an advertisement at the fort, and which hung there until the last two or three years, and which many of the citizens of Fort Benton will remember was well perforated with balls. Further investigation has brought to light the fact that X. Beidler was the commander in chief elected, and that it was his first buffalo.

Other accounts of this spectacular episode in Fort Benton history have the Indian guests sitting stoically in their circle, wondering about the antics of the White men.[29]

Chapter 5

A CODE OF HONOR
ALL HER OWN

Madame Dumont

*T*ravelers arriving on steamboats in early 1867 found a booming Fort Benton with new buildings, two hotels and many gambling establishments. In addition, frontier Fort Benton was earning a reputation featuring the "Bloodiest Block in the West," and in the summer of 1867, joints like Mose Solomon's Medicine Lodge and the Cosmopolitan were roaring with day- and nightlife of all kinds. It was from the second story of the Cosmopolitan's flimsy frame earlier in June that the notorious Eleanore Dumont, better known as Madame Dumont, left her game of 21, sprinted across the street to the levee, flourished two pistols and warned off the pilot of the *Walter B. Dance*, rumored to have smallpox aboard.[30]

Just after his arrival on the *Octavia* in the spring of 1867, Governor Green Clay Smith witnessed a brawl that spilled onto the street from the Medicine Lodge, featuring a discharged fireman from the steamer *Guidon* with a bowie knife and another man with a derringer. Sheriff William Hamilton arrested both men, but the absence of a justice of the peace forced their release. The fireman regained his knife and immediately confronted Governor Smith, who proceeded personally to subdue the man with a club.[31]

It was in this rugged frontier environment that Madame Dumont opened her Cosmopolitan in the Bloodiest Block opposite the steamboat levee in Fort Benton.

If "luxury" existed in the boisterous frontier river port of the 1860s, it was found in the gaudy hurdy-gurdy houses, saloons and gambling dens along the Bloodiest Block. The Cosmopolitan of 1867–69 was Madame Dumont's

Left: Madame Dumont, aka Madame Moustache, operated the Cosmopolitan saloon in Fort Benton's Bloodiest Block in the West from 1867 to 1869. *Author's collection.*

Below: Madame Dumont sprinted across to the levee, flourishing two pistols, and warned off the pilot of the *Walter B. Dance*, reported to have smallpox aboard. *Author's collection.*

"Pretty soon Madame Mustache and the sheriff came stomping down to the landing, both of them with guns in their hands. But it was the woman who did the talking and she did it straight from the shoulder.
"You get the hell out of here with that boat,' she said, 'and you do it pronto. I ain't going to let no smallpox spoil my business.'"

A portion of a model showing the Cosmopolitan in Fort Benton's Bloodiest Block in the West, operating night and day during steamboat season. Model at Museum of the Upper Missouri. *Author's photo.*

idea of luxury. Open from morning to morning, her saloon and gambling hall catered to the round-the-clock traffic during steamboat season from early spring through the summer. After low water ended steamboating and overland freighting hauled the last of the mountain of cargo from the levee, Madame Dumont wintered in Helena.

A small woman, olive skinned, with short, dark, curly hair, Madame Dumont dressed in elegant satin gowns, with jewels sparkling, and as she entered middle age, she was still most attractive to men. She was a woman of decisive action. She spoke well, without profanity and with a delightful French accent. She made it a house rule never to gamble with anyone except those who wished to play for high stakes and who showed up front that they had the gold dust to back up their bets. She allowed no gunplay, no fights, no loud arguments and no drunkenness. An old miner's saying was doubly true in her establishment: "Many's the miner who'd never wash his face or comb his hair if it weren't for thinkin' of the sportin' girls he might meet in the saloons."

Known to be a Union sympathizer during the Civil War, Madame Dumont allowed none of the sectional discussions that so often ended in fistfights and shootings. She was admired in the community for managing a good, honest business, without operating a house of prostitution. Madame Dumont knew Montana Territory and its miners and adventurers well, having operated in Bannack during the winter of 1862–63 and then Virginia City at the height of the vigilante activities. Sheriff Henry Plummer, dressed as a gentleman, was a patron at Madam Dumont's, as was vigilante lawman John X. Beidler. X. came not to drink or gamble but to overhear secrets revealed by whiskey-loosened lips in conversation.[32]

There are plenty of tall tales about Madame Dumont (a.k.a. Madame Moustache) and her establishments in Nevada, California, the Black Hills and Montana Territory, and these stories are legendary and entertaining, whether true or not. Yet it seems just one source provides details about her time in Fort Benton. Only one man left accounts of his visits to the Cosmopolitan and encounters with Madame Dumont there: Captain Louis Rosche, who served as first mate on the small sidewheel steamboat *Lacon* during trips to the Upper Missouri in 1868 and 1869.

Captain Rosche's biographer, journalist Robert A. Hereford, wrote a "confession" to the captain in these words:

I must confess that when I first listened to your stories—yarns you called them—as we sat in the cool, dark, high ceilinged living room in St. Louis, that I was at first inclined to take the remarkable tales with a grain of salt. I believed them to be the creations of the imagination of an old man who had plenty of time to daydream—the story of the remarkable Madame Moustache who ran the gambling hall at Fort Benton, Mont.; of Jenny [or Jennie] the neighbor girl with the beautiful golden hair, from whom the Indians lifted a piece of scalp the size of a silver dollar…and many others.

Then gradually, after months of research, I began to understand that the spectacular adventures had taken place, that you were supplying first-hand information about, telling the inside story of, a never-to-return, glamorous period of American history!

Robert A. Hereford[33]

With this introduction, here are some of Captain Louis Rosche's remarkable adventures on the Upper Missouri during 1868, as serialized in the *St. Louis Post-Dispatch*:

All kinds of women traveled up and down the river in those early, rough days, and the river wasn't very good to some of them. There was the case of Jennie. One summer I read a curious advertisement in a St. Louis newspaper. I can't remember the exact words, but it read something like this: "Wanted—young men and young women for jobs in Helena, Mont. Passage free on specially chartered boat. Will buy dogs and cats." There were directions about reporting for further information to the boat clerk.

You see, the mining city that mushroomed as the result of the rich gold strike at Last Chance Gulch was having growing pains. Young men and young women were needed to work in the stores, because most of the male population was busy trying to get rich by prospecting for gold.

The rats were bad in Helena, it seems, and that's the reason those cats and dogs were needed. Cash was paid for them, and ambitious youngsters in St. Louis turned a neat penny by rounding up stray mongrels and tabbies and selling them "up the river."

The advertisement attracted my attention, first, because I was a riverman, and second, because just about that time I had shipped again in the mountain trade. I heard Madame Moustache had set up one of her gaming houses at Fort Benton, and I decided to satisfy my curiosity to see her by shipping again on the Lacon *for Fort Benton.*

One of the young women who took advantage of the free passage to the gold fields was a girl from my neighborhood in St. Louis. Her name has slipped my mind, but we'll call her Jennie. Jennie had long, straw-colored hair which fell around her in a golden cloud almost to her knees.

Late one afternoon in August we tied up the Lacon *at a small woodyard in a wild part of Montana to refuel. I measured off 50 cords of the cottonwood logs, and I didn't have to tell those roustabouts a second time to get a move on. The Sioux were getting restless, and the Negroes had heard the stories of their attacks on steamboats. The* Lacon's *master [Captain Jake Sedam], however, was in no hurry to leave. He decided to tie up at the bank to remain overnight and told the woodyard boss of his plans. The latter, a giant whose right cheek bulged with a squid of tobacco, shook his head vigorously.*

"Captain," he said, "safest place for your boat and its passengers is right out in the middle of the river—most specifically since you got women aboard."

The Lacon's *master grinned. "Well I never pass up a chance to hear one of those massacre yarns. Let's have it." The woodyard boss shook his head. "What I'm going to tell you is no yarn. Those Sioux surprised a woodyard about 25 miles up the river and burned down the stockade and killed and scalped every one of the men and several of the women. We heard about what had happened and went up there to see if anybody was left alive. There was just one, and she was more dead than alive. She was the cook for the outfit. Captain, you say you're from Missouri and you want to be shown. You follow me, and I'll teach you a lesson that may make you change your mind about tying up here and risking the lives of your passengers."*

The Captain turned to me. "Come along, Mr. Rosche," he said, "this man has me so scared I'm afraid to go by myself." The woodyard boss said

Steamboat landing at a woodyard on the Upper Missouri, by artist Robert Morgan. *Author's collection.*

nothing but led the way through the gate of the stockade, a circular fencelike structure, fashioned of logs about 10 feet high and sharpened at the end. We entered a log building which had three rooms; one served as a dining room and living room for the woodcutters, another as the kitchen, and the third as the bunk room. Our guide led us to a cot in the far corner of the living room. A slender form was outlined underneath a sheet. I saw it was that of a woman, her head wrapped in blood-soaked bandages. The Captain was not grinning now.

"So there ain't no sich thing as an Injun massacre, eh?" the woodyard boss was saying and there was a kind of awful triumph in his tone. "Well, jes' step up a little closer and see for yourself the mess them red devils made out of a beautiful young woman."

I steeled myself, walked up to the bed, and looked loosely at the drawn, white features. To my dying day I will regret that look. "Jennie!" I gasped.

The woodyard boss looked at me in surprise. "You know her, eh?"

"She lived on our street in St. Louis," I said. "She had the most beautiful head of hair I've ever seen." I looked again at the bloody bandages. The man read my thoughts. "They didn't take off all of her hair," he said. "I guess that's why she's still alive. They skinned off a patch of scalp about the size of a silver dollar. The braves wear the scalps on their belts. A

66

woman's scalp, especially when she's got a fine crop of hair like that one there, would get in their way when they're running through the underbrush. So, they just carved off a switch and hung it on their belts…"

The girl was too far gone to recognize me. There was nothing I could do for her. I was glad to get away from that place and the Captain was also. He didn't say a word, just walked out of that log house to the boat and gave orders to move away from that spot. When we left, we had five new passengers with us. They were woodchoppers from the woodyard, and they were on their way to Fort Benton for a spree. Those woodchoppers lived a dangerous life in a wild country, and they could lick their weight in wildcats any day. Sometimes they would stay at work for six months at a stretch and, when they finally went to town they really cut loose. I said to myself, "Here are five sure customers for Madame Moustache," and I found out that I was right after I talked to one of the woodchoppers. He was a little, fried-up old fellow, with watery blue eyes but as tough as shoe leather. He had a habit of punctuating his talk by exclaiming, "Well, bust my britches!"

"You know," he said, "I'm a dead set-up for those gals in the city, and they always gets my money one way or another. It will be right pleasant to meet up with this gambling lady who anyway gives you a sporting chance to keep your coin."

"I guess you mean Mme. Moustache," I said. "I made this trip just to see her and try my luck in her gambling house. I hope she's still in Fort Benton."

"Oh, she's there, all right. Bust my britches. I can promise you that! You see the Madame is a heap sight better prospector than most of the miners who came to her joint. They say she is always the first to know when the gold veins are running thin—she can tell by the size of the bets."

"You seem to know a lot about her," I probed.

"Well, I ain't ever seen the Madame, but I've heard a heap about her, and that's why I aim to have a little game of cards with her myself. I play a pretty good hand of vingt-et-un ['21'], and I've got $500 in my poke, that it's taken me 10 years to save. I figure if the cards are running right, I can maybe run it into $5000. That'd be enough to buy a little farm I've had my eye on back in Iowa. Bust my britches if it wouldn't!" The little woodchopper leaned over and said confidently, "That $5000 is as good as mine, that is, if I can stay away from the bottle. There ain't a man gambler livin', much less a skirted one who can skin me at vingt-et-un—when I'm sober."

"They say she was quite a looker when she first showed up in Nevada City, but I reckon the Madame is getting on in years now. I understand that was back in 1854, and she was about 25. Folks say she's a French

woman. The way I've heard some tell it, she hailed from New Orleans, and she's a 100 percent Creole. Some say her real name is Eleanore Dumont…"

Business was good at the establishment of Madame Moustache. A steamboat had tied up at Fort Benton that afternoon, and a steamboat always brought customers eager to try their skill in the gambling house of one of the frontier's most famous women.

As I crossed the mud-rutted street, the noise reaching my ears was a mixture of honky-tonk piano, boisterous laughter, the clicking of dice and the rattle of the roulette ball. My heart was beating a little faster as I pushed open the doors of the weather-beaten two-story frame building and stepped into the gambling hall.

I picked out a table in a corner and sat down to get my bearings. I noticed a square platform in the middle of the room with a single table on it. The table was empty although men were gathered about several other tables. Some of these men had girl companions, and they were drinking and smoking and playing cards.

The medley of laughter, clinking glasses, and the sounds of the gambling table equipment suddenly died down, and I glanced quickly towards the door. If I had not seen the unbelievable black brush on the woman's upper lip, I would not have known that this was the famous Madame Moustache. She was fat, showing unmistakably the signs of age. Rouge and powder, apparently applied only half-heartedly, failed to hide the sagging lines of her face, the pouches under her eyes, the general marks of dissipation. Her one badge of respectability was a black silk dress, worn high around her neck. I closed my eyes in disgust.

The Madame walked to the platform, sat down at the table, picked up a deck of cards, and began shuffling them, her rings flashing as she did so. Two large raw-boned men, six-shooter holsters swinging from their hips, strolled up and leaned on a post directly behind her. I knew that they were bouncers. This was the moment that I had looked forward to for years, and yet I had little stomach for it now. I was tempted to call it quits and save my $200, but I walked to the table and sat down. I took out my leather purse and emptied out its contents of bills, gold, and silver on the table.

"Ma'am," I said, "there's more than two hundred dollars there. Let's get going now, and I don't want to quit until you've got all my money or until I've got a considerable amount of yours." I noticed the Madame's brown eyes for the first time and saw that they at least, remained youthful. She studied me thoughtfully and said, "The young steamboat officer is very practical. What shall it be, young man? Name the play."

"MA'AM," I SAID, "I DON'T WANT TO QUIT UNTIL YOU'VE GOT ALL MY MONEY OR UNTIL I'VE GOT A
CONSIDERABLE AMOUNT OF YOURS."

Captain Rosche joins Madame Dumont at the gambling table. St. Louis Post-Dispatch,
June 18, 1943.

*I didn't play any kind of cards well enough to have a choice. I saw
her eyes light up. "Very well then, it shall be vingt-et-un." I remembered
that my woodchopper friend had said this game—twenty-one—was her
favorite, but it made little difference to me. It would be painful to exhume
the memories of the hour that followed. When it was all over and my bills
and gold and silver pieces were stacked neatly in front of the Madame, I got
up, returned my empty leather purse to my pocket, and started to leave. "No,
no, no," said my hostess, waving her hands excitedly. "The steamboatman
must not go before he has had his drink on the house. Jake," she called,
turning towards the bar, "bring over the special drink."*

*"I don't want a drink," I said shortly. "I'm not thirsty." I saw the two
men who had been lounging against the post suddenly straighten. "Pardner,"
one of them drawled, "the Madame wants to set 'em up, and I believe it'd
be healthy for you to let her do it."*

I had a thirty-eight-caliber revolver in my hip pocket, but I knew that I would have no chance against the two armed bouncers, both would be expert gunmen. Just then the barkeeper placed a glass on the table, and I saw to my astonishment that it was filled with milk.

"Your special drink, Mr. Steamboatman," said Madame Moustache. Her face was sober, but there was a mischievous gleam in her eyes. That was how I first learned of the Madame's famous milk drink. I later found out that it was her custom after trimming a sucker to set him up to a glass of milk.

The little act had attracted an audience, and the guffaws of the men and the giggles of the girls didn't help to soothe my feelings.

Then a wild shout, a cross between an Indian war whoop and the blast of a showboat calliope, sounded near one of the doors. The cause of the disturbance was none other than my woodchopper friend. He and his four companions were marching towards the platform, waving their hats in the air, and whooping at the top of their voices. It was plain that the little woodchopper had not kept his resolution to "hide the bottle."

I understood what my little friend had meant when he boasted of his ability at vingt-et-un while sober, because he certainly was the world's worst player when drunk—and there was little doubt about him being that.

Every time he lost a hand to the Madame, which was just about every time one was dealt to him, he would laugh uproariously, take a swig from a bottle he carried on his hip, and shout, "Bust my britches if the lady gambler ain't cleanin' me out!"

The inevitable didn't take long. Soon all the little man's money and that of the other woodchoppers had been transferred into nearly stacked piles in front of the Madame. The little woodchopper turned his pockets inside out one by one and climbed onto the table and stood teetering there.

"Gen'men," he shrieked until the din died down, "I wanna tell one and all this is the proudes' moment of my life. I've been cleaned out by Madame Moustache. Bust my britches, gen'men, the drinks are on me."

I realized that the little fellow's invitation was made in good faith but was impossible of fulfillment because he had lost his last cent. Madame Moustache saved the situation. "I'll not allow this gentleman to treat," she said. "The drinks are on the house."

The little woodchopper, still mounted on the table, eyed with disgust the glass of milk that was brought him. "The last time I drank that stuff," he shouted, "I sucked it through a nipple!"

The Madame picked up a handful of bills from one of the fat piles. "Tell me, gentlemen, how much will your return passage be? No matter how much it is, I will see you get back from where you came."

But the Madame had misjudged her men, rather her man. "Bust my britches if I'll take any money from a woman, not even from a moustached half woman!" the little woodchopper shouted. "We must make our play, and the best man won, blast my britches if she didn't!"

His reference to the Madame's lip adornment was an unfortunate one. Her smile faded swiftly, and I saw the two armed bouncers step forward. I had an idea. "Here," I said loudly, "I've got a proposition to make. I'll make a deal with you men. I'll arrange with the captain for you to work your passage by chopping fuel for the boat."

"That's a man's proposition, that is," the little fellow shouted delightedly. "Hooray for Mr. Rosche—there's a man, bust my britches!"

That was the last time I ever saw Madame Moustache. The strange woman died as spectacularly as she lived. On a September day in 1879 her body was discovered lying in a road near Bodie [California], *where she operated her last gaming house. A poison bottle lay at her side. The night before, a gang of professional gamblers had broken the bank in her vingt-et-un game. They apparently also had broken her heart.*[34]

Chapter 6

MORE THAN A WAR CHIEF
OF THE PIEGAN BLACKFEET

A Tribute to Little Dog

F ort Benton lies in the heart of Blackfoot country. A walk on Fort
Benton's Historic Levee Trail alongside the Old Fort Benton Trading
Post passes signs paying tribute to the Blackfoot Confederacy and
one of its greatest leaders, Chief Little Dog, as follows.

BLACKFOOT CONFEDERACY

*The Blackfoot Confederacy, the Niitsitapi meaning "the real people," is the
historic name for related Nations that make up the Blackfoot Indigenous
people: Kainai (Blood), Siksika (Blackfoot), Piikani (Northern Peigan)
and Pikuni (Southern Piegan).*

*Historically, the peoples of the Confederacy were bison hunters and
gatherers following seasonal rounds across large areas of the northern Great
Plains, the shortgrass prairie ecological region. Once horses and firearms
were acquired in the early 1700s, the Blackfoot used these to expand their
territory. They followed the bison herds as they migrated between what are
now western Canada and the U.S., as far north as the Bow River and
south to the Yellowstone River.*

*Today, three Blackfoot First Nation tribes (the Kainai, Siksika, and
Piikani Nations) reside in the Canadian province of Alberta, while
the Blackfeet Nation (Pikuni) resides on the Blackfeet Reservation in
northern Montana.*

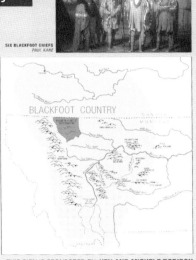

The Blackfoot Confederacy

The Blackfoot Confederacy, the Niitsitapi meaning "the real people," is the historic name for related Nations that make up the Blackfoot Indigenous people: the Kainai (Blood), the Siksika (Blackfoot), the Piikani (Northern Peigan) and the Pikuni (Southern Piegan).

Historically, the peoples of the Confederacy were bison hunters and gatherers following seasonal rounds across large areas of the northern Great Plains, the shortgrass prairie ecological region. Once horses and firearms were acquired in the early 1700s, the Blackfoot used these to expand their territory. They followed the bison herds as they migrated between what are now western Canada and the United States, as far north as the Bow River and south to the Yellowstone River.

Today, three Blackfoot First Nation governments (the Siksika, Kainai, and Piikani Nations) reside in the Canadian province of Alberta, while the Blackfeet Nation (Pikuni) resides on the Blackfeet Reservation in northern Montana.

SIX BLACKFOOT CHIEFS
PAUL KANE

BLACKFOOT COUNTRY

THIS SIGN IS SPONSORED BY: **KEN AND MICHELE ROBISON**

Blackfoot Confederacy sign located near the entrance to Old Fort Benton Trading Post. *Author's photo.*

LITTLE DOG

The people of Fort Benton had no better friend among the Blackfeet Nation than the Piegan chief, Little Dog, who advanced to the leadership of his tribe by a succession of brave exploits in war, and wise decisions in tribal councils. He was described by those who knew him as of splendid physical bearing, intelligent, proud, and of great integrity of character.

As a relative of Natoyist-Siksina Culbertson's he was a frequent and welcome visitor to the American Fur Company's trading post Fort Benton. For over twenty years the company depended upon Little Dog to maintain the good will of the Blackfoot for their business. He was mainly responsible for keeping their trade from going to the Hudson Bay Company. He not only sought peace with Euro-Americans but also between Indian nations.

At the 1855 Lame Bull and 1865 treaty negotiations, Little Dog performed excellent service by inducing the Blackfoot to see the wisdom of accepting the terms and conditions offered by the U.S. government. His

Piegan Blackfeet Chief Little Dog

The people of Fort Benton had no better friend among the Blackfeet Nation than Piegan Chief Little Dog, who advanced to leadership of his tribe by a succession of brave war exploits and wise tribal-council decisions. He was described as being intelligent and proud, having great integrity and splendid physical bearing. As a relative of Natawista Culbertson, he was a frequent and welcome visitor to the American Fur Company's Fort Benton trading post. For more than twenty years, the company depended upon Little Dog to maintain the good will of the Blackfeet for their business.

Ultimately, however, his friendship with Euro-Americans brought about his death. Certain members of his tribe to developed a feeling of distrust toward him. On May 27, 1866, Chief Little Dog was ambushed and murdered by a small group of Piegan. He was killed on the Cracon du Nez trail near the Teton River northeast of Fort Benton. His son, Fringe, who came to the defense of his father, died with him. Both were buried in the original Fort Benton cemetery, then located just west of the trading post.

THIS SIGN IS SPONSORED BY: **KEN AND MICHELE ROBISON**

Sign honoring Blackfeet Chief Little Dog, collocated with the Blackfoot Confederacy sign. *Author's photo.*

friendship for Euro-Americans brought about his death. Certain members of his tribe succeeded in creating a feeling of distrust toward him among his people. On May 27, 1866, Chief Little Dog was ambushed and murdered by a small group of Piegan led by Isadore, along the Cracon du Nez trail near the Teton River. His son, Fringe, who came to the defense of his father, died with him. Both were buried in the original Fort Benton cemetery then located just west of the trading post.

LITTLE DOG, A WHITE FRIEND

The Blackfoot Nation, after a deadly conflict with Meriwether Lewis in 1806, regarded Whites with hostility, as early trappers found. In 1830, at Fort Union, Kenneth McKenzie made, in effect, a "peace treaty" that permitted the American Fur Company to establish a trading post on the Upper Missouri River in Blackfoot Country for mutual benefit. That truce

While no image of Chief Little Dog exists, this is an image of his descendant Little Dog and his wife by N.A. Forsyth. *OHRC.*

extended only to employees of the successive trading posts: Piegan (1831), McKenzie (1832), Lewis (1845) and Fort Benton (1846). Independent trappers remained fair game, and the Blackfoot raided far and wide.

Among the most powerful warriors was Little Dog of the Piegan, who respected the peace with the American Fur Company but, about 1845, led a party that wiped out a migrant train near Fort Hall on the Oregon Trail. Taken in that raid was a chest of what the Piegans thought were brass buttons without holes. Little Dog cached the box under rocks, later to learn that the "buttons" were gold pieces. Yet he never returned for them.[35]

Greatly impressed by the daunting numbers of Whites moving west, Little Dog concluded the best course was friendship. Thereafter, Whites had no better friend. He was one of the first signatories to the 1855 Lame Bull treaty at the mouth of the Judith River and the first to sign the 1865 treaty.

A relative of Natoyist-Siksina Culbertson and a friend of the Culbertsons, Little Dog was a frequent visitor to Fort Benton and a trusted friend of later post traders Andrew Dawson, Matt Carroll, George Steell, John J. Healy and A.B. Hamilton. Another trader, Bill Hamilton, once credited Little Dog and his son, Fringe, with saving the lives of his party. Chief Little Dog agreed to the peaceful transit of the Mullan Military Wagon Road Expedition through Blackfoot Country in 1860, and he aided Agent Alfred Vaughan in establishing the Blackfoot Experimental Farm north of Sun River Crossing. Little Dog saved many White lives during the Sun River Stampede of 1865–66. Importantly, he repeatedly interceded to alleviate the growing tensions between settlers and freighters and the Blackfoot during the 1860s.[36]

Healy Knew Little Dog's Courage

Irish adventurer, Fort Whoop-Up founder and Choteau County sheriff Johnny Healy related this story of the remarkable courage of his friend Chief Little Dog:

> *Little Dog had a son* [Fringe] *who was the father's counterpart in personal appearance and possessed the reckless courage and remarkable intelligence of his parent. It is said, and I have personal knowledge of more than one instance in proof of the assertion, that these two men were, in deadly encounter, more than a match for ten of the best warriors of the tribe, and such was the confidence felt in their skill and prowess that a war party under their command would follow them into the very jaws of death. I will relate one instance to show the sort of stuff these two Indians were made of.*
>
> *A war party of Piegans, consisting of twenty well-armed and mounted men, had encountered six Assinaboine* [sic]. *The latter had taken shelter in an Indian war house, a structure built of logs and affording a strong and safe defense to those within.*
>
> *After fighting all day, the Piegans were unable to take the fortification and would probably have withdrawn from the contest after the sun went*

down. But towards evening, Little Dog and his son attracted by the firing, came up, and learning that the war house was defended by only six men, they laughed at the Piegans, calling them cowards and squaws, and without a moment's hesitation dashed up to the fort, in the face of a deadly fire from those within, leaped over the logs, killed four of the defenders and dragged the remaining two by the hair out of the fort and turned them over to the squaws to be put to death.[37]

THE TRAGIC DEATH OF CHIEF LITTLE DOG

Certain members of Chief Little Dog's tribe developed a feeling of distrust toward him for his attempts to maintain friendship with Whites. On May 27, 1866, Chief Little Dog was ambushed and murdered by a small group of Piegan as he was returning to camp from Fort Benton. He was killed on the Cracon du Nez Trail near the Teton River, north of Fort Benton. His son, Fringe, died with his father. Chief Little Dog and his son were buried west of Old Fort Benton.

It is noteworthy and tragic that following the death of Chief Little Dog, Blackfoot-White culture clashes and warfare dramatically increased until the culmination at the Marias or Bear River Massacre on January 23, 1870. The *Montana Post* of June 9 reported Little Dog's murder:

MURDER OF LITTLE DOG AND HIS SON

The most exciting topic just at present, is the murder of Little Dog, the head chief of the [Piegans], a great friend of the whites, and of his son, by a party of drunken Indians of his own tribe. The following particulars we obtained from the principal interpreter of the tribe. It appears that several [Piegans] were in and about the Fort on the 27th ult. [May 27], their camp being…northeast from Benton. Having finished their business, they soon started for their wakiups, in small parties. Little Dog himself left only a few minutes before his son, who was the last of the party. On the road to the Marias River…the Chief, who was on foot and accompanied by one of his squaws, was overtaken by a half-breed named Isidore, who was on horseback, and reining up asked to see the old man's revolver, which was at once complied with by Little Dog, without any suspicion of danger. On receiving the weapon, Isidore told the poor,

Chief Little Dog and his son, Fringe, were killed in this vicinity on the trail from Fort Benton to the Blackfeet encampment. *Author's photo.*

defenseless old man that as his party had whiskey in a little ravine a short distance ahead of them, and as they were afraid of their Chief, he would keep the pistol.

Little Dog's remonstrances were unavailing, the half-breed coolly riding off, followed by Little Dog, whose squaw was more suspicious than her Lord, recommended a hasty retreat to Benton. The old man acquiesced, but fatally for himself, said he would get his pistol first, and instead of beating an instant retreat to the Fort, followed the thief until he came up with the drunken and still carousing savages, and demanded his weapon. They told him that he had no need of it as they were going to kill him anyhow, and without assigning any reason for so doing, they all fired upon him, killing him on the spot. Not satisfied with simple assassination, they mutilated the dead body in the most horrible manner, with butcher knives.

The dead Chief's son hearing the firing and attributing it to some quarrel, ran up, and on overtaking the squaw was told that the savages had killed his father. Being totally fearless of danger the young warrior rushed up to the scene of the bloody debauch and asked: "Who killed my father?" These words were his last, for another volley from the party stretched him lifeless beside the mangled remains of his father, and in a few seconds, he was as savagely mutilated as the old Chieftain had previously been.

The consummation of the iniquitous purpose of the Indians may be laid at the door of those who persist in selling whiskey to the Indians. Little Dog was always friendly to the whites, and lived in the Fort, the greater part of the winter. He was instrumental in making peace between the Crows and [Piegans]. This morning the aged warrior and his son were laid side by side, in the same grave. [38]

Chapter 7

THE MYSTERY AND BOLD LEGEND

General Thomas Francis Meagher

At midday on July 1, 1867, General Thomas Francis Meagher, escorted by at least six militia men, rode hard along Montana's Benton Road, down from the bluffs overlooking Fort Benton, and entered the pages of history and the portal of legends. Ten hours later, the former acting governor of Montana Territory, heroic Civil War leader of the famed Irish Brigade and Young Ireland revolutionary leader General Thomas Francis Meagher was dead—his death shrouded in mystery and his body lost to the depths and swift current of the June rise on the Missouri River. Rumors of suicide, of insanity, of intoxication, swirled in the aftermath.

After attaining heroic stature during the Civil War, General Meagher came to frontier Montana as territorial secretary and became acting governor on the departure of Governor Sidney Edgerton in 1865. The brilliant—but brash and unpredictable—secretary and acting governor, with his wife, Elizabeth, were the center of the social and political scene of the new territory during these booming placer gold mining days. Revered in Fenian Irish and Democratic circles, Governor Meagher fought political battles with the strong Lincoln Republican faction. The arrival of newly appointed governor Green Clay Smith in the fall of 1866 relieved Meagher of many of his demanding duties. However, Smith left the territory in early 1867 to escort his family up the Missouri River to Fort Benton, and Meagher again took on the demands of acting governor.

General Meagher, hero of the Irish Brigade during the Civil War, served as secretary and acting governor of Montana Territory. *Author's collection.*

By the spring of 1867, Montana Territory faced an expanding settler population and a rising threat from Indian nations responding to the rapidly increasing White presence. Ever hard-charging, General Meagher called for federal troops, only to be answered by a promise of a federal arms shipment to the new army post Camp Cooke on the Missouri River. Meagher determined to go to Fort Benton either to receive the arms there or to engage a steamboat to go down to Camp Cooke.

Acting S departed Virginia City about June 17 accompanied by his militia escort. He arrived in Helena on June 19, spent several days there and left for Fort Benton in ill health about June 22. The next day, on the Benton Road, the general met Governor Smith, who was returning with his family after their June 20 arrival on the steamboat *Octavia*. During their brief meeting, General Meagher relinquished the governorship. Having recently been replaced as territorial secretary, Meagher was without employment and pondering his future.

By the evening of June 23, General Meagher and his escorts had arrived at Johnny Healy's trading post at Sun River Crossing. Meagher was suffering from severe dysentery, perhaps a symptom of more serious medical problems. In the words of Meagher biographer Paul Wylie, "Years of drinking and the rigors of his chaotic life had taken their toll." For the next week, Meagher remained at Healy's post recovering from his ailment. A week with colorful Irishmen Healy and Meagher and others, no doubt drinking and swapping tales of the Montana frontier, must have been something to behold. The evening of June 30, a blacksmith working for Huntley's Stage Line reported enjoying an evening supper "laughing and joking" with General Meagher's party at Healy's little twelve-by-twelve-foot log dugout trading post.[39]

Early the next morning, July 1, General Meagher and his escort departed for Fort Benton and, after hard riding, arrived tired and dusty around noon. The view they saw from the bluffs overlooking Fort Benton is hard to imagine. The head of steamboat navigation on the Missouri River in the 1860s meant just that. During the year 1867, forty-one steamboats departed St. Louis and, after the long, 2,400-mile trip through snags and rocks and sandbars, arrived at the Fort Benton levee between May 25 and August 8. These mountain boats, 150 to 250 feet in length, carried an average of two hundred tons of freight, bringing a total of more than eight thousand tons to the Fort Benton levee.

At the Fort Benton levee that day were four steamboats, all sternwheelers: the *Amaranth*, *G.A. Thomson*, *Gallatin* and *Guidon*. The *Amaranth*, commanded by Captain James Lockhart, had arrived two days earlier, bringing 225

General Meagher left Virginia City for Fort Benton to meet an arms shipment from the federal armory. This box, addressed to "His Excellency the Governor of Montana Terr.," is on display at the Museum of the Upper Missouri in Fort Benton. *Author's photo.*

General Meagher rode from Sun River Crossing to Fort Benton with his militia escort on that fateful day, July 1, 1867. *Anaconda Standard.*

tons and 12 passengers to Fort Benton. The *G.A. Thomson*, under Captain J.M. Woods and pilot John T. Doran, had landed the previous day with 200 tons cargo and 68 passengers after a long, hard, 67-day trip from St. Louis, suffering damage from a minor collision en route. The steamer *Gallatin*, under Captain Sam Howe, had arrived at the levee earlier on the morning of July 1 with a load of government freight from Camp Cooke but no government arms. The *Guidon*, commanded by Captain James L. Bissell, acting throughout the boating season as tender on the Upper Missouri, had arrived on June 20 with 225 tons and 57 passengers plus an additional 130 passengers from Camp Cooke who had been stranded by the earlier sinking of their steamboat, *Nora*. The *Guidon* was moored astern the *G.A. Thomson* at the Fort Benton levee on July 1.

Two other recent steamboats had just departed the Fort Benton levee. The *Ida Stockdale*, commanded by young Captain Grant Marsh, had arrived on June 29, with twenty passengers from the *James H. Trover*, which was grounded on a bar forty-five miles below the mouth of the Musselshell. Another noteworthy boat, the *Octavia*, under Captain Joseph LaBarge, had arrived June 20 with a cargo of 174 tons and seventy passengers, including Governor Smith and his family. The *Octavia*'s trip had been marred by the murder of an English nobleman, Captain Wilfred D. Speer of the Queen's Guards. Speer was shot point-blank in the head by U.S. Army sentry Private William Barry, an Irishman and part of a contingent of one hundred soldiers from the 13th Infantry Regiment en route to Camp Cooke. The *Octavia* had departed Fort Benton downriver on June 25, although the murder of the Englishman was still the talk of the town, and the incident added to the animosity and ever-present tension between the Irish and the English.

Some eight hundred tons of freight had arrived on the levee during the past week. Part of this massive cargo had been loaded on wagons and was already moving along the Benton Road, but several hundred tons remained on the levee. Many wagons and men and hundreds of oxen, mules and horses were loading, unloading and moving from the levee through the streets of Fort Benton and onto the trails leading in every direction therefrom. From four to eight yoke of oxen drew each wagon, which could carry about two tons of freight. Each wagon train made a stunning show.

The sleepy little river town of today was booming and bustling day and night during the steamboating season in 1867.

Adding to this rough frontier environment, tensions had risen with Native Americans during recent months, reports had come of the latest

Fenian invasion of the British possessions the previous year and territorial political and social antagonisms had increased. As General Meagher rode into town, weighing heavily on his mind, no doubt, was the fact that he was in debt, out of work and the subject of immense controversy, beloved by many, hated by others.

Republican leader and political adversary of Meagher Wilbur Fisk Sanders was present in Fort Benton awaiting the arrival of his family, who was coming up the Missouri on the steamboat *Abeona*. Sanders greeted General Meagher and his escort and spent part of the early afternoon with him. Fort Benton merchant I.G. Baker met the general on the levee and invited him to midafternoon dinner at Baker's house across from the levee. During their conversation, General Meagher announced that he was going downriver to receive the arms shipment.

General Meagher spent much of the afternoon before dinner next door in a back room at Baker's store where he read, greeted visitors and wrote correspondence. It was there that Meagher wrote his last letter, imploring territorial auditor John Ming to pay back wages due to ease his serious financial woes.

After spending the early afternoon at the I.G. Baker store and eating dinner at Baker's home, Meagher boarded the steamboat *G.A. Thomson*

During his last afternoon, General Meagher spent time in the back room of I.G. Baker's store greeting visitors, reading and writing his last correspondence, a plea to the territorial auditor for back pay. *OHRC.*

General Meagher ate a late afternoon "dinner" at the home of trader I.G. Baker. Built in the early spring of 1867, this wood-frame home encased adobe construction, as seen in this 1880s photo. *Author's collection.*

to spend the night. After being settled in the captain's cabin, Meagher was never seen again, and his body vanished in the depths of the spring rise. Did he die by vigilante justice? Trip and fall from a damaged railing? Jump in frustration over failed finances and his failing health? That is the great mystery of General Meagher's death in Fort Benton and the heart of the legend.[40]

Paul R. Wylie's *The Irish General* carefully sorts through the conflicting stories of the general's last day. Wylie explores the accounts of Wilbur Fisk Sanders, I.G. Baker, pilot Johnny Doran and others and examines possible suspects ranging from vigilantes to anti-Irish hotheads to Meagher's enemies such as Indian agents Augustus Chapman and Major George B. Wright. These accounts, conflicting often in detail and tone, make fascinating reading. Wylie also weighs the evidence for an act of suicide or a tragic accident to explain the death. Since the law was not sufficiently established in Fort Benton at the time, no coroner's inquest was held. Author and lawyer Wylie filled this void by composing a sketch, "Coroner's Inquest into the Death of General Thomas Francis Meagher,"

The historic I.G. Baker home has been maintained and is open to the public. *Author's photo.*

and presented it to the Fort Benton community on the weekend of the dedication of the Meagher Monument on the old steamboat levee. The inquest, held just five days short of 142 years after Meagher's death, was performed on Friday evening, June 26, 2009, with testimony by a role-playing cast.[41]

After sorting through the conflicting evidence, here is this author's conclusion. During the afternoon on July 1, General Meagher was sober but still suffering from severe dysentery. I.G. Baker offered Meagher several glasses of blackberry wine, commonly used then to cure diarrhea. Meagher enjoyed a late-afternoon dinner at Baker's home. Toward dusk, Meagher sat with a group of men in front of Baker's store. The party got loud, and Meagher began exhibiting possible symptoms of delusion and paranoia, expressing concern that his enemies were about to do him harm. Doran escorted Meagher to the steamboat *G.A. Thomson.* There, Meagher, Doran, James M. Woods (captain of the boat) and others began drinking in the boat's salon, and Meagher became inebriated. Doran eventually got the general into the cabin of Captain Woods, the exterior door of which faced

2000 DOLLARS
REWARD!!

Proclamation by the Governor!

Helena, Montana Territory,
July, 5th. 1867.

Information having been received by me, that the body of General Thomas Francis Meagher has not been recovered from the Misouri river, and it being desirable that the same should be done, in order to proper and christian burial ; now therefore, I, Green Clay Smith, Governor of Montana, do offer a reward of One Thousand Dollars (\$1000) for the recovery of the said body, and its safe delivery at Fort Benton, St. Louis or either of the Military Forts on the Missouri river, where it can be procured by friends.

In testimony whereof, I have hereunto set my hand and the great seal of the Territory, this, the day and date above written, and the Independence of the United States of America, the ninety-first

GREEN CLAY. SMITH,
Governor of Montana Territory.

At a Meeting of the Citizens of Helena, held on the evening of the 4th day of July, 1867, the following Resolution was unanimously adopted :

RESOLVED, That N. P. Langford, Esq., Chairman of the Meeting, be, and he is hereby authorized—in behalf of the citizens of Helena—to offer an additional Reward of One Thousand Dollars, for the same purpose.

Now, therefore, in accordance with said Resolution, I do hereby offer a reward of One Thousand Dollars, (\$1000,) pledged by the citizens of Helena, in meeting assembled, for the recovery of the body of

GEN. THOMAS FRANCIS MEAGHER,

And its delivery at either of the places designated in the foregoing Proclamation of Governor Green Clay Smith.

N. P. LANGFORD, Chairman.

Attest :
PETER RONAN, Sec'ry.

Rocky Mountain Gazette Job Print, Helena, Montana.

Broadside reward for recovering General Meagher's body, offered by Governor Green Clay Smith. Rocky Mountain Gazette, *July 6, 1867.*

the river. Meagher got ready for bed, and Doran, thinking his friend was at last sleeping, left him and proceeded to the lower deck.

About ten o'clock, Doran heard a splash in the waters and heard the cry of "man overboard," uttered by the boat's Black barber, who was on watch and had caught a glimpse of a man plunging into the river from the cabin deck. Most likely, General Meagher, dressed in his underclothes, suffering from exhaustion, too much to drink and diarrhea, opened the cabin door to proceed to the stern of the boat to relieve himself. Along the way he stumbled and fell overboard from the deck, likely where part of the deck guard railing was missing from an earlier collision.

Several witnesses in addition to the night watchman saw a body fall from the boat. One credible witness, Ferdinand Roosevelt, Wells Fargo agent at Fort Benton, saw Meagher fall overboard and testified that there was no attacker and that General Meagher had been drinking heavily. A correspondent from the *Montana Post* was on board the steamer *Guidon* at the time; he heard the plunge and briefly saw a head in the water, then all was still. Another credible witness, Private Eugene Tucker from the 13th Infantry Regiment at Fort Shaw, wrote to his parents:

> *I have nothing of importance to write but on the first of July when down to Benton Gen. Meigher* [sic] *committed suicide by jumping in the river, you have no doubt seen in the papers that he accidentally fell overboard but as I was not more than 50 feet from him at the time. I know better, for he had a fit of delirious trembles.* [42]

Pilot Doran described the waters as "certain death, as the river there was about 12 feet deep and with a current rushing at the rate of nine miles an hour." [43] Floating lifebuoys were put out, lights were lit, a boat was launched and every exertion was made first to rescue and later to recover the body of the general. The search continued for several days before it was called off. Meagher's would not be the first or the last body never to be found after drowning in the "Big Muddy." General Meagher's body was lost to the ages, but his spirit lives on.

On hearing the news, Governor Smith issued a proclamation ordering a tribute of respect and offering a reward for recovery of Meagher's body. Flags of General Meagher's native land and adopted country were flown at half-mast as a mark of respect to his memory. A large "citizens' meeting" was held in Helena to mourn the general's death, proclaiming, "Our country has lost a true patriot, a friend of universal liberty, a sympathizer with the

In 2009, this tribute to General Meagher was rededicated on the grounds of the Montana state capitol by a large crowd including Montana's Hibernians. *Author's photo.*

afflicted of all nations, a foe to tyranny, a fearless and intrepid general, a man of genius and of eloquence, who, at all times was ready to sacrifice personal interest for the public good."[44]

Ironically, Fort Benton returned quickly to normalcy with steamboats coming and going with regularity. The *G.A. Thomson* left for St. Louis at noon the next day, July 2, "with some twenty passengers, the majority of whom were returning pilgrims, disgusted with the country."[45] Fort Benton "had a gay time" on the Fourth of July."[46] At noon, all available ordnance in the town "belched forth the joyous proclamation of the only American national holiday." At two o'clock on board the steamer *Antelope*, a large audience assembled to listen to the "finest, most terse and appropriate" Fourth of July oration by Colonel Sanders, preceded by the reading of the Declaration of Independence by Major Wright. In the evening, the celebration was closed by "a squaw dance in a large hall on the levee, well attended by all shades of female aborigines, most of whom, although well versed in the arts of the mazy dance, resisted all attempts at conversation, astonishing St. Louis gentlemen, who honored the floor with their fashionable selves."

Monument honoring Meagher on the historic levee at Fort Benton, adjacent to where he mysteriously drowned after falling from the *G.A. Thomson. Author's photo.*

Innumerable fights occurred, and "the inhabitants enjoyed themselves as well as could be expected under the circumstances." By then, the search for General Meagher's body had been suspended.[47]

In a letter from Fort Benton dated July 6, "Fleet-Wing" (an otherwise unidentified Benton news source) reported that the *Gallatin* had arrived that evening and landed a battery of 6 twelve-pound mountain howitzers, 2,500 stand of muskets and an immense amount of ammunition for the use of the Montana militia.[48] General Meagher's arms had arrived, but he was not there to meet them.

As you visit today's Fort Benton, you see a small, quiet river town with a big history. Look over Fort Benton from the bluffs and imagine the town in 1867 going full blast night and day during steamboat season. Imagine the long levee crowded with up to eight steamboats at a time, hundreds of tons of freight piled on the levee, and hundreds of freight wagons and muleskinners filling the streets and departing for trails radiating from the head of navigation in every direction.[49]

When you walk the streets and tour the ancient I.G. Baker adobe home, imagine the Irish general sitting there, eating his last dinner with Baker. As you read the interpretive sign on the levee, imagine General Meagher sitting at a table in the back room of the now-demolished Baker store spending his last afternoon. As you visit the Museum of the Upper Missouri, look at parts of two surviving crates addressed to "His Excellency the Governor of Montana Territory" and used to ship the very arms from the federal arsenal at Frankfurt that arrived after the general was lost. As you walk the levee, imagine General Meagher greeting Sanders and many well-wishers. Envision the two-hundred-foot steamboat *G.A. Thomson* moored alongside and General Meagher fevered and restless in his stateroom just before he stepped out the cabin door and off the deck into the cold, swirling current to his watery grave. Pause at the Meagher Monument on the levee to pay homage to the exceptional Irish revolutionary hero, the brave Civil War leader of the Irish Brigade and the larger-than-life early Montana territorial saint and sinner. Today, Meagher is honored from Waterford, Ireland, to Fort Benton, the final stop on the Meagher mystery tour!

Chapter 8

WHAT A WAY TO TREAT A LADY!

Libby Meagher's Rocky Ride Downriver

Geneneral Thomas Francis Meagher lived life on the edge, and he continues to attract international interest, with followers from Waterford, Ireland, to Tasmania drawn by his colorful life and his tragic and mysterious death in Fort Benton on the night of July 1, 1867.[50] Yet despite the general's enduring fame, little has been written about his wife, Elizabeth, and the few words that have been written about her time in Montana Territory are rife with inaccuracies. Elizabeth "Libby" Meagher came up the Missouri River to join her husband in the Territory of Montana in 1866. A year later, in June 1867, Libby is supposed to have gone to Helena on her husband's fateful trip to Fort Benton, but didn't she really remain in Virginia City? On his death on the evening of July 1, she is supposed to have rushed to Fort Benton and spent months patrolling the banks of the Missouri, directing the search for her husband's body, but did she really? Elizabeth is supposed to have left Montana on a steamboat by the end of September to return to New York, but how and when did she really leave, and what was her trip by steamer down the Missouri River like?

Libby Meagher first arrived in Fort Benton on June 5, 1866, onboard the sternwheeler *Ontario* in company with her husband, who had gone downriver from Fort Benton to meet her. Among the thirty-eight passengers arriving at Fort Benton after the slow, fifty-seven-day trip from St. Louis were ten women and eight children; famed missionary Father DeSmet; territorial chief justice H.L. Hosmer and his family; Judge J.P. Williston and his family; Townsend Poore, superintendent of a mining company, and

Elizabeth Meagher, wife of the general, made her way from Virginia City to Fort Benton to board a steamboat for her return to New York. *Author's collection.*

his wife; Professor D.S. Henkel, a German metallurgist; D.W. Tilton of the territory's first newspaper, the *Montana Post*, and his family; and merchant Matthew Carroll.

The June 16 *Helena Radiator* announced, "The Acting Governor, General Thomas Francis Meagher arrived from Benton, with his better half, on yesterday. We welcome her to her new Mountain home, and may she find in it, all that her heart desires." After several weeks in Helena, where they participated in Fourth of July celebrations, Elizabeth Meagher and her husband moved on to their residence in Virginia City, the territorial capital. They settled into the social life of the bustling capital of Montana Territory.

Elizabeth Townsend Meagher was thirty-six years of age when she arrived on the Montana frontier. She had married the brilliant Irish exile in New York and accompanied him for the rest of his life, often serving as secretary and later as nurse. She was with him at the First Battle of Bull Run early in the Civil War and nursed him back to health after he was wounded. It would take more than the remote Montana frontier to separate them. General Meagher and his lady lived in Virginia City, and their small log home was a social center there.

Thomas Francis Meagher was a brilliant lecturer, Irish hero and territorial official, serving as secretary and part-time acting governor, with many social and political demands. By the spring of 1867, acting governor Meagher was facing an expanding settler population and a perceived threat from Indian tribes, especially in southern Montana. His calls for federal troops were answered by a modest shipment of arms destined for Camp Cooke on the Missouri at the mouth of the Judith River. Meagher determined to go to Fort Benton either to receive the arms there or to embark a steamboat to go down to Camp Cooke. Meanwhile, Libby Meagher remained at their home in Virginia City.

General Meagher's tragic death in Fort Benton on the night of July 1 shook the young territory and launched the legend of controversy and mystery.

So, what about grief-stricken Libby Meagher? Prominent historian Robert Athearn writes: "For nearly two months after the death of her husband, the

The Meaghers' modest residence in Virginia City. *Library of Congress.*

grief-stricken daughter of wealthy old Peter Townsend pathetically patrolled the tawny banks of the Missouri, searching for her husband's body….When fall came to Montana that year, she reluctantly abandoned the search and returned to New York."[51]

Historian Gary Forney concludes, "Elizabeth immediately came to Fort Benton where she reportedly walked the banks of the Missouri River, and employed others as well, in an extended search for the body of her husband. By the end of September, Elizabeth abandoned the search for her husband's remains and returned to New York City to live again in her father's home."[52]

So, did Libby Meagher rush to Fort Benton and patrol the banks of the Missouri for months searching for her husband? What a great story, but is it true? The absence of any mention in either the Helena or Virginia City newspapers of Mrs. Meagher's quick departure for Fort Benton argues against the story. There is simply no evidence that Libby Meagher came to Fort Benton before her sad departure from Montana Territory by steamboat on September 2.

If, as appears most likely, Libby was in Virginia City at the time of her husband's death, then she would have learned the tragic news about July 5. If she had departed immediately for Fort Benton, she would probably have arrived there about July 10. Yet there is evidence in the *Montana Post* that Mrs. Meagher was in Virginia City on July 26 to receive a petition from the Fenian Brotherhood. There is simply no known evidence that Libby did rush to Fort Benton. The Fort Benton reports carried in the territorial papers did not mention her arrival. Not one word appeared in either the *Helena Herald* or the *Montana Post* about her departure. Libby Meagher simply did not rush to Fort Benton, and she did not patrol the banks of the Missouri for months or even days.[53]

Elizabeth Meagher did make her departure from Virginia City on August 16. The *Montana Post* announced:

> *Mrs. General Meagher left yesterday* [August 16] *per private conveyance for Benton, thence by river for the East. It was with sincere regret our citizens bid good-bye to this most estimable lady, and her friends in Montana will ever cherish her memory fondly. Quite a few* [of] *the citizens turned out in Nevada and formed an escort of honor, while overhead the twin flags of Erin and Columbia floated out on the breeze.*[54]

On her way to Benton, Libby Meagher arrived in Helena on August 18 and spent the next ten days bidding a sad farewell to friends in that city. Since the steamboat *Gallatin*, the last boat to leave Benton for the States that season, was scheduled to depart on the thirty-first, Mrs. Meagher likely left Helena on Tuesday morning, the twenty-seventh, for Fort Benton.

Libby arrived in Fort Benton on August 29 to board the *Gallatin*. No record has been found of how she spent the days in Fort Benton waiting for the departure, but she no doubt had an outpouring of support from the small community, especially among the strong Irish contingent—there were only five White women in Fort Benton at this time. No doubt I.G. and Fannie Baker welcomed her to their small adobe home.

The Virginia City *Montana Post* on August 31 gave Libby Meagher a fine sendoff tribute:

> *Homeward Bound.—Mrs. Meagher takes passage on the steamer Gallatin, advertised to leave this day for St. Louis. The following from the pen of*

Miles O'Reilly is a deserved tribute to her who leaves our Territory to-day, and, perhaps, forever: "How noble a wife she has been—with what fidelity of warm devotion she has clung to the varying fortunes of her brilliant but erratic lord—only those could tell whose lips must remain silent under the seal of social relationship. Reared in luxury, and as much flattered and followed for her beauty as Meagher has been in early days for his genius and gift of eloquence, she never faltered in her allegiance to the exile who reached his highest fortune when he won her heart. Whither he went she followed him; his people became indeed her people, and his God she made her God. We dare not write more upon this branch of the subject, though we write from an overflowing heart, and have many thoughts surging upward and clamoring for expression." [55]

Finally, on Monday, September 2, Elizabeth Meagher began her sad journey home to New York, a trip that would prove long and difficult. The steamboat *Gallatin* departed Fort Benton for Omaha, with Elizabeth Meagher and 149 other passengers and upward of a quarter of a million dollars in gold dust onboard. After trouble from late-season low water, the boat reached a point thirteen miles below Camp Cooke on the morning of the fifth. Here, the *Gallatin* ran hard on the rocks at Holmes Rapids, and for six days, the crew and passengers worked with block, tackle and spars,

The ill-fated steamboat *Gallatin*, with Elizabeth Meagher onboard, departed Fort Benton late in the season. *OHRC.*

struggling to get it afloat. On Sunday, September 8, the steamer *Only Chance* came along, and about twenty-five of the *Gallatin's* passengers gave up and took passage down on that boat, an action they would later regret.

By Wednesday September 11, the *Gallatin's* crew and passengers had strained and racked the boat so severely that it was considered unsafe to remain onboard any longer. All the passengers and freight were put ashore and the boat dismantled, even to the deck planking. Its splendid machinery was left in place, in hopes it might eventually get through, and the steamer was tied to the bank. Later passenger accounts spoke highly of the conduct of Captain Howe, who worked day and night in the cold weather and water to save his boat and secure comfort for the passengers.

The lady passengers and children—including Elizabeth Meagher and Mary (Mrs. James F.) Berry with her three-year-old, Jennie Lee, and twin baby girls, Anna Natalle and Adelaide Price—along with their provisions, baggage and a few male passengers, were put onboard two mackinaw boats. The balance of the passengers started overland on foot to reach the steamer *Huntsville* at Cow Island, fifty miles below. Eight miles downriver, the mackinaws met Captain Jacobs of the *Huntsville*, coming up with a yawl to their relief. He agreed to carry passengers on the *Huntsville* to Omaha for seventy-five dollars in currency, while Captain Howe of the *Gallatin* generously gave all the provisions he had and all the money left from the trip.

Having no cooking utensils, the mackinaw party, including Elizabeth Meagher, laid down to sleep about eleven o'clock that night, rather hungrier than was pleasant. To add to their discomfort, the rain coldly and continuously poured down on them through the night, with wolves howling in the distance. Berry family legend tells that Elizabeth Meagher had plenty of buffalo robes and shared them with Mary Berry, who wrapped her six-month-old twins in the robes, saving their lives.

After an early start, the mackinaws reached the *Huntsville* by ten o'clock in the morning, while the foot passengers, hungry and weary, wet, footsore and demoralized, came struggling in by squads until night, thankful for their deliverance from a boat wreck on the Upper Missouri.

The money and provisions from Captain Howe left $21.50 due from each cabin passenger and $6.00 from each deck passenger, which was paid. The *Huntsville* then waited for the arrival of the ship's clerk and additional travelers from Fort Benton.

Boating conditions in that late season were horrible. The steamboat *Imperial* was hard aground twelve miles below Cow Island on September 14, with poor prospects of getting off. Another boat, the *Zephyr*, was above

Cow Island and, it was believed, would have to remain all winter in the mountains. The *Only Chance* had a terribly rough trip down to Cow Island, pounding over rocks all the way. It left Cow Island on September 12 and made its way down to Omaha, the passengers, including the twenty-five from the *Gallatin*, suffering all the way from poor-quality food leading to much sickness and two deaths from dysentery. One passenger recorded that "a gladder set of boys never walked a steamboat plank" on their arrival at Omaha on October 4.[56] Onboard were over two hundred passengers and about $3 million in treasure.

The steamboat *Huntsville* with Elizabeth Meagher and the Berry family aboard departed Cow Island on September 19. The boat passed Fort Peck on the twenty-eighth and worked its way down the Missouri, slowed by the late-season low water, the almost constant need to spar across sand bars and frequent high winds. At long last the *Huntsville* arrived at Omaha on October 17. The Berry family continued to their home in Mexico, Missouri, by train after their life-threatening trip down the Missouri River. The sad journey ended for Mrs. Thomas Francis Meagher as she boarded a train for her family home in New York, but the legend of General Thomas Francis Meagher was just beginning.[57]

Chapter 9

HIDDEN STORIES

The Vigilantes of Fort Benton

While the books about vigilantes imposing frontier justice on Montana's gold mining camps likely could fill the hold of the steamboat *Luella*, little has been written about the vigilantes in frontier Fort Benton. Was that because vigilante justice in Fort Benton didn't exist, or is it because the early vigilantes imposed greater secrecy? There was no editor Dimsdale or a *Montana Post* operating in Fort Benton at the time.

Certainly, there was little legal law and order in the 1860s, and during the spring and early summer steamboat season, Fort Benton was among the liveliest and most lawless towns in the West. The "Bloodiest Block in the West" was booming day and night with an intensity far beyond the reaches of law and order in any form. And it wasn't until 1869 that the frontier army had a continuous presence at Fort Benton, leaving a void in military protection against horse raids and other incursions by Native war parties.

The office of sheriff featured a revolving door, with a dozen sheriffs serving Choteau County between 1862 and 1870. Even in the early 1870s, four sheriffs held office, and often the sheriffs during that Whoop-Up period were themselves stampeding across the Medicine Line to open a trading post.

THE MANY SHERIFFS OF TERRITORIAL CHOTEAU COUNTY

1862	James Stuart	Based in Bannack, Washington Territory, which included Choteau County.
1863	Jeheil B. "Buzz" Caven	Based in Bannack, newly created Idaho Territory; served only for a few weeks.
1863	Henry Crawford	Based in Bannack.
1863–64	Henry Plummer	Based in Bannack.
1865	A.B. Hamilton	Appointed. First sheriff resident at Fort Benton.
1866–67	William T. Hamilton	X. Beidler named William Hamilton sheriff in 1866.
1867	George Croff	Appointed.
1867–68	Asa T. Sample	First elected September 1867. (Per the *Montana Post*, June 5, 1868).
1868	John B. Morgan	Appointed. Died November 8, 1868.
March 1869	John Buckmaster	Appointed. (Per the *Montana Post*, March 5, 1869.)
June 1870	J.D. Weatherwax	Per the 1870 U.S. Census, Montana, Choteau Co., Fort Benton.
1870–72	Henry A. "Fred" Kanouse	Per the *New North-West*, October 21, 1879.
1872–75	Trevanion "Van" Hale	Elected sheriff. His obit states that he served three terms as sheriff in the 1870s (not confirmed). Resigned in June 1875 because of his involvement in the Cypress Hills extradition trial.
1875–77	William "Billy" Rowe	Appointed July 1875; elected August 1875; resigned June 1877.
1877–82	John Jerome Healy	Appointed June 1877. Elected in 1878, defeating Van Hale; defeated Rowe in 1880. Lost election in 1882.

1882–86	James McDevitt	Elected.
1886–88	William Harvey Black	Elected.
1888–94	Benjamin F. O'Neal	Elected.

The first word of a "vigilance committee" at Fort Benton appears in Deputy Indian Agent Hiram D. Upham's report of February 2, 1866, to the commissioner of Indian affairs in Washington, D.C. Upham wrote from Fort Benton:

The white men on the bottom [Fort Benton] have lately organized themselves into a kind of vigilance committee for self-protection against both Indians and whites. All [Blackfoot] war parties have heretofore made it a practice to stop here on their way to and from the enemy's camp. They have always been welcomed by their French and half-breed brothers-in-law.[58]

FORT BENTON VIGILANTES DISPENSED CRUDE JUSTICE

Thus, from early on, Fort Benton had a vigilance committee for protection against both Native and White lawlessness. In the face of such an environment, and in the absence of legal law and order, vigilante justice happened in secrecy under the societal surface. In some cases, the presence of a local committee is reflected by just a hint, such as a letter from a traveler to Fort Benton in the *Montana Post* in June 1866 describing a vigilante poster prominently displayed in town:

This organization has a branch at Fort Benton, we presume, for a neatly written little poster conveyed the following terse and significant warning to belligerents:
  "BEWARE. The Vigilance Committee is in session. Beware of the careless use of firearms. B order."
  The good folks of Benton, it seems, are determined to have order and peace among them, at all hazards, and are prepared to maintain it themselves, until civil law shall afford them protection from the acts of the lawless.[59]

THE *LUELLA* THEFT INCIDENT

The warning poster appeared at the very time the steamboat *Luella*, under Captain Grant Marsh, arrived at the Fort Benton levee on June 17, 1866. Captain Marsh's biographer Joseph Hanson described the environment in the river port and an incident onboard the *Luella* that triggered vigilante action:

> *At the time of Captain Marsh's first arrival, the feeble arm of the new territorial government had not yet gained strength to reach from Virginia City to Fort Benton, and here the Vigilance Committee still ruled supreme. The men composing it did not meet in formal conclave to debate the punishment of a suspected offender. A few low words spoken in passing as they met each other on their daily business, a vote taken in the same manner, and perhaps the next morning a still figure would be found hanging by the neck before one of the stores, or some hulking individual would have disappeared from his familiar haunts never to return, fled in the night from a grim warning he did not dare question or resist. The law of the Vigilance Committee was stern and uncompromising, but it was seldom unjust, for even the extremity*

The steamboat *Luella*, under Captain Grant Marsh, brought down from Fort Benton the largest shipment of gold dust on record, worth some $2.5 million ($46 million today). *OHRC.*

of its punishments found excuse in the chaotic conditions of frontier society.

In Fort Benton so great had become the terror inspired by its constant menace of swift vengeance upon evil doing, that Captain Marsh saw men ride in from the mines, fling down their saddles, with sacks of gold dust tied to the cantles, upon the floor of Baker, Carroll and Steell's store and go away for a week's spree, to find when they sobered up and returned that their property had not been touched.

While the Luella was unloading, one of her deck hands stole from the cargo a box of patent medicine, doubtless because the nostrum contained a large percentage of alcohol. In some way the vigilantes learned of the theft.

Grant Marsh, captain and pilot of the steamboat *Luella*, the greatest steamboat man on the Upper Missouri. *OHRC.*

The miscreant was tried by one of the mysterious tribunals and the next night was seized and borne away to a secluded spot where he was whipped until nearly dead. The captain afterward was informed that the Vigilance Committee had come within three votes of returning a verdict for hanging the thief, but the punishment accorded was sufficient, and no more petty pilfering occurred on board the Luella.[60]

A BROAD VIGILANTE REACH

The broad reach of the Fort Benton Vigilance Committee is reflected in the swift and harsh retaliation against Native Indian raids during the winter of 1865–66 along the Benton to Helena Road and against the Blackfoot Government Farm and abandonment of St. Peter's Catholic Mission just as it was being established in a new location near the Mullan Road south of the Sun River Valley.

A dozen Benton men, including John Morgan (a later sheriff), John Neubert and Joseph Pearson, rode eighty miles, killed one Piegan and caught and hanged three others. This series of raids and vigilante responses fueled the increasing Native-White conflicts, on the verge of becoming a "Blackfoot War," that only ended after the tragic massacre of Chief Heavy Runner's camp on the Marias River in January 1870.[61]

Many years later, Joe Culbertson, son of Fort Benton founder Alexander Culbertson, wrote that he lived in Fort Benton from the late 1860s until 1872, when he relocated with his father to Fort Browning. Joe wrote about the vigilantes' activity, noting that their headquarters in Fort Benton was the store of Matthew Carroll and George Steell.

BILL HYNSON:
THE DESPERADO WHO HELPED HANG HIMSELF

Joe Culbertson was present and likely a witness at the most outrageous vigilante action in Fort Benton—and the only recorded hanging. He described the environment at the time:

X. Beidler, U.S. deputy marshal, frequent visitor to Fort Benton and Montana vigilante hangman. *Author's collection.*

Fort Benton was one of the toughest places, outside of Whoop Up country, that there was in the territory of Montana. It wasn't unusual to have one or two killed every other night in Fort Benton. Front street was all saloons except for three log trading stores [including] Carl and Steele [Carroll & Steell], headquarters for the Vigilantes....I was living in Fort Benton when Bill Hynson, marshal for Fort Benton, dug his own grave and bought the rope for the vigilantes to hang him. X Beidler, vigilante, planned this necktie party in 1868.[62]

Long before Fort Benton hosted a hometown newspaper, news from the rough frontier town filtered through the territory's first newspaper, the Virginia City—and later Helena—*Montana Post*. The *Post* of August 28, 1868, brought the news of this vigilante hanging in Fort Benton:

HANGING AT BENTON—At Benton, on Monday night [August 24], Col. Geo. Hynson was hung by parties nominally unknown. A hoisting apparatus was constructed of four rails, set on end, and with their tops fastened together, and between these Hynson was found hanging on Tuesday morning. The charge against him was for highway robbery and a general bad character. It is said that when he first came to the country, he came in

Model of 1860s Fort Benton's Bloodiest Block with saloons and dance halls offering returning miners one last chance to leave their gold dust during an exciting night before they boarded a steamboat to return to the States. *Author's photo.*

> *company with a full set of burglar's tools, and he is thought to be the person who strangled and robbed the China woman in this city* [Helena].

The same page of the *Post* corrected the identity of the hanging victim—it was not Civil War veteran and upstanding citizen of Virginia City George W. Hynson but rather desperado William Hynson.[63]

> *THE HANGING AT BENTON.—The unfortunate individual who was recently hung at Benton was Wm. Hynson, instead of Geo. Hynson as recently reported by us. He is a young man, a native of Missouri, aged about twenty-eight years, who came here some two years ago, and who has not borne a very good character during his sojourn in the Territory. Last summer he stole the rifle of the Hon. W.H. Claggett from the Blackfoot coach and is supposed to be the one that murdered [China Mary] last winter. He has recently been employed as a watchman on the levee at Benton.*
> *A few nights before he was hung, he is said to have knocked down and robbed a freighter. The fact that he obtained but two dollars by this proceeding did not lessen the magnitude of his crime in the eyes of the people at Benton, and his case was, therefore, without his knowledge, examined by a committee. His execution being determined upon, the committee informed Hynson that they were about to hang someone and wished him to help them. In compliance with their request, he bought the rope and assisted in the erection of the primitive scaffold which afterwards served for his hanging. His body was allowed to hang nearly two days before he was cut down.[64]*

THE TRUE STORY

While the *Montana Post* corrected the identity of the victim and provided sketchy details, the full story did not emerge for several decades. The hanging was not forgotten and provoked much discussion over the years. What had Hynson done to incur the wrath of the Fort Benton vigilantes? How was he convinced to help with his own hanging? Clarity was needed, yet a half century passed before the complete story emerged in the *Conrad Independent* in 1918 with a most intriguing headline:

Murderer Who Was Marshal of Fort Benton Dug His Own Grave and Bought the Rope With Which Vigilantes Hanged Him

Old timers who lived at Fort Benton in the 60s, few of whom are left today, used to indulge in a knowing smile whenever the name of Bill Hynson came up in conversation. For many years the fate of Hynson was a subject that always provoked much discussion and many arguments, but the solution of the mystery of his death and the strange circumstances surrounding it have never been published.

The curious fact about Bill Hynson's death was that he erected his own gallows, dug his own grave—or at least superintended the digging of it, and bought the rope with which he was hanged. No other criminal of pioneer times who was the victim of Vigilante justice ever did more in assisting the territory to rid itself of his presence....

It was in the spring of 1868 that Bill Hynson came to Fort Benton from Helena, where he was suspected of being a murderer and was known to be a robber....

Beidler tried to find evidence sufficient to convict Hynson of the Chinese woman's murder, but was unable to do so, and he was forced after a time to release Hynson. The latter soon left Helena, and the following spring, in 1868, the two met on the streets of Fort Benton when Beidler returned from Whoop-Up country. Hynson had undoubtedly intended to kill Beidler, but the latter accosted the murderer on the street and bluffed him out. [65]

Nathaniel Langford describes this meeting in his *Vigilante Days and Ways*:

Hynson and Beidler approached each other in the street. The former extended his hand in a friendly manner, which Beidler seized with his left hand, keeping his right in reserve for the use of his pistol.

"I am told," said Beidler, "that you have come here to kill me."

"I kill you!" said Hynson, in well-affected surprise.

"Yes, you," said Beidler, dropping the hand he held; "and if you wish to try it, you'll never have a better chance. If that's what you want, you can't pull your pistol too quick."

Hynson glared at the little, athletic man who confronted him so boldly, and saw in those burning eyes and that steady muscle not the smallest trace of fear.

Seizing Beidler again by the hand, he said in hurried tones,—"X., I did make a fool of myself when drunk in camp with the boys, in some remarks relating to you, but I didn't mean it. I don't want to hurt you, and never did. Now, let's be friends."

Beidler, who had no other feeling than contempt for the bragging poltroon, listened in silence to what further he had to say.

"I want you," said Hynson, "to aid me in getting the position of night-watchman in this city."

X. replied to this request in general terms, and, turning on his heel, left Hynson, who afterwards, by some means which X. could not fathom, received the appointment he desired. [66]

As night watchman, Hynson committed many crimes of thievery and appropriating valuables that came into his possession as an officer of the law.

HYNSON DIGS OWN GRAVE

Hynson was suspected of crimes, but he was always shrewd enough to act without leaving evidence that might convict him. However, Beidler and the better citizens at Fort Benton watched and waited.

On the morning of August 18, a Fort Benton businessman, whose name has never been made public, went to Hynson, and with an air of mystery told him that there was a man who needed hanging in the town and that a party of prominent residents had decided to quietly execute him that night.

"Who's going to be the star at this hanging bee?" inquired Hynson with much interest.

"Hush," said his informant, "I am not at liberty to say, but we want you to be present and take part in the execution."

Hynson acquiesced willingly, for an enterprise of this character was greatly to his liking. "Say," he suggested, "let me get the rope, select the place, and have the grave dug. I'll have everything fixed by tonight."

The other man smiled and said: "All right, Hynson. You go right ahead and make the arrangements. We want you to be right with us."

THE END OF HYNSON

A little later in the day Hynson was seen driving a wagon containing three pine tree poles to a secluded spot on the prairie near the town. The poles were about 12 feet long and four inches in diameter. Tying one end of these three poles securely together, he raised them up in the form of a tripod. Then, whistling cheerfully, he went to a store and purchased a small coil of rope.

"What's that for?" inquired a bystander.

"To hang a man with," replied Hynson with a laugh. The bystander thought this a good joke and let it pass as such.

Hynson next hired a negro [Henry Mills] to go out with him and help dig the grave. When the colored man reached the spot and saw the arrangements, he nearly turned white with terror.

"Who's dead, Massa Hynson?" he inquired.

"Never mind," replied Hynson. "You keep your mouth shut and help me get this grave dug. I'll furnish the corpse."

Before the afternoon was spent the grave was dug.[67]

In the early evening, Hynson got the rope, and a few citizen vigilantes—including X. Beidler, who happened to be in Fort Benton—made their way to the temporary gallows. When they got to the execution site, Beidler snatched the rope from Hynson and tossed the noose around his neck. The condemned man made a hard struggle but was overpowered and hauled up the tripod. The job was not an artistic one, as Hynson's toes did not quite clear the ground so that he slowly strangled to death.[68]

The next morning an Indian brought the news downtown that a white man had been hanged. The people flocked out to the spot. When the vanguard arrived, they saw the ghastly face, with protruding tongue and lifeless eyes staring at the morning sun, was that of Bill Hynson, night marshal of the town.

Presently [Henry Mills] came, who had helped dig the grave. When he recognized the swaying form beneath the tripod, he gasped:

"Fore God, dat's Bill Hynson. He done tol' me to help dig de grave and said he'd furnish de corpse!"

"Well," remarked a bystander, "he made his word good, didn't he?"[69]

After the body was cut down, there was found in a pocket the following letter from the mother of Hynson:

"My dear Son,—I write to relieve my great anxiety, for I am in great trouble on your account. Your father had a dream about you. He dreamed that he had a letter from your lawyer, who said that your case was hopeless. God grant that it may prove only a dream! I, your poor, broken-hearted mother, am in suspense on your account. For God's sake, come home."[70]

Who hanged Bill Hynson? There used to be a group of old timers at the head of navigation on the Missouri who smiled in a knowing way whenever the question was asked. Also, it may be said, X. Beidler might have thrown some light on the subject. But no one talked.

CIVIL WAR VETERAN JAMES LOWELL ARRIVES

In August 1869, James Howard Lowell arrived in Fort Benton. Following Civil War service in the Union army, during which he was severely wounded at Antietam, Lowell traveled west, mining a while in Thompson Gulch, and eventually came to Fort Benton, intending to return to his home in Kansas. Instead, Lowell lingered for two years, becoming a valued member of the community by practicing law while serving as deputy district attorney and county assessor. In his memoir, edited by Katherine Squires, Lowell recorded intriguing commentary on the local vigilantes.[71]

VIGILANTE VENGEANCE FOR BOWLEGS

In the spring of 1871, a Frenchman known as Bowlegs walked up behind the Blackfoot wife of Baptiste Racine and shot and killed the baby boy on her back. Bowlegs was jailed, then taken by a group of residents one night from the jail, armed and informed he had a running start on the vengeful father. Bowlegs took off on the run. Racine followed. No spectator admitted to more than hearing a yell and a shot, but Baptiste Racine was the survivor. The April 7, 1871 *Helena Herald* confirmed the incident with a terse "Bowlegs, in jail for murdering a little girl, was taken by a crowd, not heard of since."[72]

James Lowell played a key role in this tragic Bowlegs affair and recorded it in his memoir:

> *I was reading in my den when I heard the loud screams of a squaw holding in her arms a papoose, which she brought over her shoulders, with a bullet hole across and through its temples. It took quite a bit of arguing to learn how it happened, and this is the story. This woman and another were in a cabin, and a drunken half-breed entered and, after frightening remarks, drew his gun and fired. I was then acting deputy district attorney and filed with the probate court an information against the man whose name was the French one of Pipeneaux Wypert [aka "Bowlegs"].*
>
> *He had taken to the brush and for more than a year was not within our jurisdiction. He turned up one day and I got out a warrant and he was put in the jail. This jail was some three hundred yards in the oblique rear of the courthouse and was made of staunch logs.*
>
> *It was probably a few nights after, and after commitment, that I heard sounds from my quarters in the wing of the courthouse coming from the direction of the jail. Stepping out into the shadow I noted a body of men at the jail door, I recall as yesterday, the rising of the moon and lighting up the scene.*
>
> *I saw the leader and heard the conversation. The jail door was broken open, and Pipeneaux was led out. The father of the slain papoose, whose name I have forgotten [Baptiste Racine], was there. The preliminaries were talked over and arranged. The Master of Ceremonies prescribed with much ability what was to be done. Papineaux was given a certain number of paces, which the Master stepped off, and the parent was given free scope to follow him. Pipeneaux asked for a pair of moccasins. This indulgence was granted.*

The pursuer was given a Henry rifle, and at a given signal, the Master, who had placed Pipeneaux, called the word. The moon had risen and lighted the level of mingled sagebrush and low thorn that stretched a mile and more toward the fort. It was not a duel; it was a gauntlet run. Thrice wounded, Pipeneaux sunk down and expired within a quarter mile of his start.

The men moved away to the halls, save one, I saw him—the Master—go alone to the body of Pipeneaux and fire his revolver into him. The crowd had dispersed and following the last function of the Master of Ceremonies, I walked to the halls to see him and the confederates as easily and demurely plying the vocation there as if nothing of importance had interrupted the game at the tables.

Lowell continued his account of vigilante action while at Fort Benton.

MORE VIGILANTE ACTION AVERTED

It is not to be denied that order and a respect for the law were not entirely ignored [in Fort Benton]. *No indeed, the crucial point between lawlessness and order may have been overstepped, but not for long. Benton was never dangerously overridden during my stay there, I mean, unredeemedly so. A vigilance committee was thought necessary, and its organization comprised a resolute minority; an executioner of the committee's decisions was a member. He was the Master of Ceremonies where Pipeneaux Wypert was given a chance for his life.*

It happened this way. The winter of 1871 had nearly depleted the town. Off on hide and fur quest, and a large party to the British dominions had diminished the residents. They were away to make a stake, as it was called. The town was practically dead—the boating season over—and nothing really to do. Our hangers on levied tribute on the merchants and got a subscription of $200 per month to parade and night watch the town.

It was during this period that an incident occurred. On the range, some small herds of cattle—few in number compared with the herds of later years—sometimes these small herds were the prey of marauding Indians. In one of the herds, the owner noticed a loss of three or four taken one at a time. This was considered a White Man's business. Below Benton and near the Fort was a slaughterhouse, and anchored in the river near its beach, held down by rocks, were found the hides of the missing beeves branded and certain of identification. This meat plant was owned and operated by one named W.S. Stocking, with whose family—a most estimable people—I boarded.

One evening, entirely ignorant of the circumstance related, I was passing a corridor where the telegrapher, [S.V.] Clevinger, held forth, and my attention was arrested by sounds in Clevinger's office of loud talk. This was then the rendezvous of the order of Vigilantes. My knock, though recognized, admitted me with some forcible insistence on my part. The reason was quite plain. These were some men of character and standing there, but my landlord, Stocking, was to all appearances to be victimized, the evidence against him seemed to have no defensive feature, or the basis for a plea in his behalf, except the hearing was ex parte. On this point, I took up the cudgel, and to my surprise, moderated the feeling as against the "Executioner" who had seemingly got hold of those present with his extreme notions of dealing with accused persons; the result was that I was appointed a committee of one to warn Stocking to leave town within ten hours. I have a letter from Stocking written in his hiding that followed the order of the Vigilantes. It is only fair to remark that Stocking claimed that an enemy of his planted the hides in the river at the junction of his slaughterhouse, and I have no reason to disbelieve his statement.

That night after the adjournment, I went to my quarters in the solitary wing of the courthouse after leaving the house of Stocking, where I delivered the message. I could not rest or sleep and watched from the windows— gun in hand—for the man whom I had denounced in plain terms at the meeting of the Vigilantes. The next day, passing up the riverfront, came towards me the man: he offered a gentlemanly greeting—and more, he proffered assistance should I ever need it from him. It is that a microbe was taken out of me. He was skilled in the art of immediately presenting an absent gun. Among his maxims was, "If you see a man looking for trouble, accommodate him." I stood once at a bar with him and others, he raised his two forefingers apart and said, "Hills never come together, but men may," then brought his fingers together.[73]

THE MASTER OF CEREMONIES

Regrettably, Lowell does not name the mysterious leader of the vigilantes, yet he described him in respectful terms.

The Master of Ceremonies was not a dime novel desperado, no more courtly gentleman was there. He had none of the airs of the bully; his antecedents were unknown and in that little community he was held more in fear than in detestation, and as far as I know, he was never guilty of striking down any who did not deserve it. White, not Indian. In the tragedy of Pipeneaux Wypert, he gave the accused moccasins and distance between him and the fatal rifle....He had to him a justification as a promoter of the peace.

James Lowell ends his discussion of the Master by revealing his death, which happened about six months after Lowell left Fort Benton in 1871:

As might be supposed, the Master's death was tragic. I have heard that while about to execute the decree of the Vigilantes upon one whose guiltiness was in doubt, he [The Master] *was seized and executed.*[74]

In an intriguing case that followed, a shooting occurred in one of the saloons in the Bloodiest Block. Saloon owner L.W. Marshall shot and killed a colorful character, Dennis Hinchey. A strikingly important letter from Fort Benton to the *Helena Herald* provides the best expressed case for vigilante justice in Fort Benton at this time when governmental justice seemed amazingly absent. Additionally, the author of the letter may well have provided a hint at the identity of the Master of Ceremonies couched in his careful terms—was the Master Dennis Hinchey?

On Sunday morning, about four o'clock, one of those unfortunate occurrences that frontier towns are not unfrequently subjected to, occurred in Marshall's billiard saloon, resulting in the death of Dennis Hinchey, formerly a citizen of Galena, Ill., but for the last three of four years of Colorado and Montana, and a somewhat notorious character of the border. Hinchey was on one of his sprees, and apparently determined to wipe out some one; when, for his own preservation, and probably that of others, Mr. Marshall, one of the proprietors of the saloon, shot him, and he is sustained by all good citizens in so doing. This affray brought to light the strange fact that the only officers of the law present in Choteau County are two Commissioners and the Assessor; no Sheriff, no Coroner, no Justice of the Peace, no Constable. I am informed that a full set of officers was elected at the last election, but most of them are at present out at Whoop-up trading with the Indians [emphasis mine]. *Now, Mr. Editor, this may be all right at Benton, but I hardly think that is what those officers were elected for.*[75]

A coroner's jury met and found that Dennis Hinchey came to his death by four pistol shots from the hands of L.W. Marshall. The case was closed quietly by a jury of twelve men, who pronounced Marshall justified in the killing of Hinchey. While we may never know whether Hinchey was the Master, his death occurred at the right time and seemed to end Fort Benton's vigilante activity. On the other hand, the departure of James Lowell from the town removed our most reliable recorder of vigilante activity.[76]

THE HOODOO BLOCK

While Fort Benton's gunfighters favored the saloons along the Bloodiest Block, a dark curse descended on the nearby HooDoo Block, where all too many tragedies occurred. The curse of the HooDoo Block lived on for many decades.

It all began with the hanging of Billy Hynson by his own rope, left swinging from the gallows he had erected well into the next day before he was thrown to rest his dark soul in the grave he had prepared. The evil legend of the HooDoo Block began that summer day in 1868.

At the time, the almost empty block featured a small log jail, the gallows and a house built by a tough character, John B. Morgan, who was sheriff at the time. Morgan also dug a well near the house and built an adobe stable and corral to open a livery business. Shortly after Hynson's hanging, Sheriff Morgan's Piegan wife died, and their house burned down—no further details are known. About a month later, the *Helena Herald* reported another tragedy:

Our Sheriff John B. Morgan died yesterday morning [November 14] *at 8 o'clock, after prolonged illness, during two weeks of which he was confined to his bed. Scarcely a month has passed since he buried his wife. He leaves five children, all under age. I was told his disease was typhoid pneumonia, he believed it to be intermittent fever.*[77]

Over the next few years, the HooDoo Block continued to earn its name as more tragedies befell it. In the summer of 1869, several wagons were attacked, and two White men were killed by Indians thought to be Blackfoot,

HooDoo Block No. 25 on Main Street, with log jail and gallows, in the 1860s, the scene where many tragedies befell early Fort Benton. *OHRC.*

later discovered to be Crow. This occurred about fifteen miles from Fort Benton, and the residents were up in arms. At this critical time, a fourteen-year-old Blackfoot youth, brother of the powerful Mountain Chief, rode into Fort Benton carrying dispatches from Major Culbertson. This boy and several companions were shot to death, and the bodies were tossed into the Morgan well. This practice continued for years, creating the legend of the Place of Skulls.[78]

On November 28, 1872, a soldier and two Diamond R muleskinners went on a drunken binge, threatening to ravage the town. They were arrested and locked safely in the jail before they could do harm to Fort Benton's property or residents. The curse of the HooDoo Block took over from there. At three o'clock the next morning, nearby residents awakened to smell burning logs and discover the jail wrapped in flames. The first on scene concluded that the prisoners had broken out and then set fire to the jail. Yet once the building was reduced to ashes and had cooled off enough to investigate safely, in stirring up the ashes, the charred skull and bones of a man were found, and this created the impression that all three of the prisoners had been roasted alive. Further search found the remains of a second man in the ashes but no portion of the third, although every particle of debris was examined and reexamined. Buttons were found in the ashes, which were recognized as belonging to the uniforms worn by the soldier and one of the other prisoners.

A belt, identified as belonging to muleskinner Frank Thompson, was found a short distance from the jail. This, coupled with the fact that no trace of a third man was found in the ashes, led to the conclusion that Thompson escaped after murdering his comrades. A search found no further clues or trace of Thompson.

Adding to the mystery of it all, the army commander at Fort Benton suppressed all information about the entire incident—the only reporting came from 13th Infantry sources at Fort Shaw.[79]

In later years, Ferdinand Roosevelt built a furniture store on the opposite corner at Bond and Main Streets. While under construction, it blew down during a terrible storm, the only building in town affected. Roosevelt rebuilt, yet the next year, the store caught fire, destroying his extensive inventory. That 1885 fire swept on to burn the newly built Odd Fellows Hall nearby. The last chapter was written when the livery burned in an apparent final burst of evil energy, leaving the block empty except for the well-stocked Place of Skulls.

The HooDoo Block stood vacant until the old stories died. In the early 1900s, new buildings went up, and in the words of historian John Lepley, "old timers agreed that the HooDoo had exhausted its power for evil."[80]

Chapter 10
VIGILANTE HANGMAN X. BEIDLER

Fort Benton's Marshal

*I*n an eloquent graveside funeral oration, the famed vigilante prosecutor Wilbur Fisk Sanders paid homage to the legendary vigilante hangman John Xelpho "X." Beidler, the man who for more than two decades brought more law and order to the Montana frontier than any other pioneer.

On January 23, 1890, X. Beidler died in his room in the Pacific Hotel in Helena. Days later, Sanders spoke of the time in the 1850s when young Beidler joined the abolitionist crusade of John Brown in "Bleeding" Kansas as slaveowners and antislavery crusaders fought a bloody rehearsal for the Civil War. In a skirmish, X. was shot and left for dead on the field—the wounds he received lamed him for life. Sanders followed X. to western Kansas, which became Colorado, and on to Bannack in then Idaho Territory in June 1863—and on to Alder Gulch where, in December, Sanders prosecuted—and X. hanged—the murderer George Ives in Nevada City. The Ives trial and hanging began the vigilante "cleanup" of Sheriff Henry Plummer's notorious gang of highway robbers and murderers in lawless pre-territorial Montana.

Sanders eulogized Beidler, this "man of brave heart," as he discharged "every duty that necessitated every hardship....He was, in my view the most unique and interesting character of our early history. His courage amounted to the highest audacity. There were no risks that he was ever asked to take that he did not do with a cheerfulness, the like of which is seldom known to be paralleled."

John X. Beidler bust with a sign for a vigilante meeting at six thirty. The sign came from Frontier Town, located for years near Helena. *Author's collection.*

Through X.'s many years as deputy United States marshal, Sanders professed:

> *He accepted all danger that came into his path and willingly accepted the consequences, whatsoever they might be.*
>
> *For about three years he was collector of customs of the port of Fort Benton engaged in the charge of preventing the smuggling of articles across our northern boundary. During a few seasons, he was in the employment of transportation companies, engaged, at great peril, in taking the treasure that was produced in Montana to steamboats and later the railroads; and he has had in his individual possession and confided to his honor for protection, millions upon millions of gold. Sanders emphasized, "He has never betrayed a trust, and in the presence of this audience, for him and for the greater portion who knew him better than any other man in Montana, I believe that I can confidently appeal to them to say that he never said of any human being an unkind word."*

Sanders spoke of the good times and the bad that marked periods in the life of his great friend lawman Beidler, concluding: "Now we are about to lay him in the beautiful valley near us and erect in bronze or marble a memorial of the gratitude of his neighbors and friends, where shall be inscribed on its base: 'Brave pioneer! To true occasions true.'"[81]

Fort Benton's "Lawman"

Through his years as deputy U.S. marshal, X. Beidler ranged widely throughout Montana Territory. Both as marshal and collector of customs, frequently and for extended periods, Fort Benton was his base of operations, taking Beidler north across the Medicine Line into Whoop-Up Country, east down the Missouri River to the Dakota border, west into Blackfoot Country and onto the streets and into the saloons of Fort Benton.

Beidler's name appears in other tales in this collection, as he protected shipments of gold dust, chased criminals of all kinds and participated in major events centered on the river port town. *River Press* editor Joel Overholser emphasized often that X. was:

A Frequent Benton Visitor

John X Beidler, a living Montana legend from Vigilante days, turns up often at Fort Benton. In the Vigilante cleanup of the Montana mining camps in 1863–64, the short and stocky 32-year-old Pennsylvanian was executive secretary (hangman)….One high point, he turned a hesitant crowd at the trial of George Ives for murder into a hanging crowd with a shouted, "Ask him how much time he gave the Dutchman." The latter was Nick Tbolt, killed for a few dollars' gold dust and his employer's mules….

Possibly his first visit to the head of navigation was in 1865 during the peace treaty….There was an idiotic stampede to Sun River at year end 1865–66. Beidler [was] among the would-be miners who was helped with food and shelter by Little Dog of the Piegans. But a few miners were robbed or killed by Blackfeet, many more died of cold, and acting Gov. Meagher was trying for an Indian war. Beidler, Wm. Berkin, and Bob Hereford came back after "organizing" Bentonites for defense….

Beidler toward fall 1866 was in charge for a Helena bank of several million dollars (two tons) gold shipments that went to Fort Benton and the steamboats that year. He reported the dust was divided into three safes, each aboard a wagon drawn by a couple of mules. Here the armed guard secured the safes to empty ten-gallon kegs and sent them downriver by mackinaw, the writer believes this shipment went aboard the Luella at Cow Island.[82]

LUELLA GOLD

As *Luella* navigated down the Missouri River, news of its massive gold cargo traveled rapidly. Leavenworth (KS) Times, *October 5, 1866.*

During the height of the Montana Gold Rush in 1866, Captain Marsh received his first command, and both the steamboat *Luella* and Captain Marsh earned accolades that year. Acting both as master and pilot, Captain Marsh brought *Luella* to Fort Benton on June 17 from St. Louis. Remaining on the Upper Missouri throughout the summer, Captain Marsh returned to Fort Benton on July 11 from Fort Union with cargo for the North West Fur Company. Captain Marsh arrived a third time on August 10 with cargo and machinery salvaged from the *Marion* at Pablo's Rapids.

The first steamboat to remain so late on the Upper Missouri, *Luella* departed Fort Benton on August 16 and dropped down to Cow Island for a September 3 departure after boarding 230 miners returning to the States. Captain Marsh piloted *Luella* down the Missouri River through water barely two feet deep with a cargo of two and a half tons of Confederate Gulch gold dust, conservatively valued at $2,250,000–$46,000,000 today. This was the richest cargo ever to go down from Fort Benton, and X. Beidler had guarded that gold dust through all dangers on its way from the mines to *Luella*.[83]

Editor Overholser continued his story:

COLLECTOR OF CUSTOMS

"X" was confirmed as collector of customs for Montana and Idaho territories in April 1867. There had been no boundary survey, nobody

knew where it was so Beidler came to Fort Benton to consult with Alexander Culbertson. They loaded trade merchandise on a couple of wagons and headed north. Up around Belly River Culbertson opined the small party was now on the British side and set up a trading post. "X" went on, soon finding an infantry company from Fort Shaw and informed them they were over the border. Then he was taken prisoner by Blackfeet who discussed varied ways to terminate his career before a friendly chief freed him.

Joe Culbertson credits "X" with being organizer for hanging of Bill Hynson here in August 1868.

DEPUTY U.S. MARSHAL

As a deputy marshal, he continued efforts aimed at curbing the U.S. whisky trade with Indians. In the fall 1868 in that capacity, he turned up at Pikuni Trading Post on Big Dry creek on the Marias to close it because Canadians were owners, along with Liver Eating Johnston and Bill Hamilton, sheriff at Fort Benton. Operator Charles Price Hubbard didn't appreciate the visit, writing that Beidler "was so crooked he couldn't hide behind a corkscrew."

It was hard times for "X", next year he was a woodchipper on the Musselshell shortly after woodhawks and wolfers had wiped out a war party of Sioux.

Al Wilkins many years later recalled "X" as headquartering at Fort Benton in 1874. "I have seen him toss a fruit can out in front of him, take a six gun in each hand and keep the can rolling until both guns were emptied." At the time he made Fort Benton his headquarters.

[As] deputy U.S. marshal much of the time his duties were in northern Montana. An 1884 diary exists, showing that he was at Mose Solomon's on the Marias in January, in February at Fort Benton to witness a flood caused by an ice jam. He entertained the pilgrims in Fort Benton saloons with tales of earlier days; in May during one of those chilly spring storms started the conversation ball rolling with "Boys, did you ever see winter set in as early as this?" Others, probably barkeep Tom Todd among them, picked up the gambit, until a few pilgrims regretted the impulse that had brought them to growing Montana territory....Next year he brought Pike Landusky in from the Little Rockies and lodged him in the Choteau County jail after Pike had attempted to kill his partner, Dutch Louie Meyer, co-discoverer of gold in that area.

And there "X" fades from the Fort Benton picture.[84]

THE REST OF THE STORY

While editor Overholser hit some highlights, the details of many other tales afford greater insight into X.'s indomitable character and courage. For instance, sampling Beidler's activities in northern Montana, in June 1867, X. was in Fort Benton, bringing several outlaws who had absconded from Diamond City in Confederate Gulch. X. seized several hundred dollars of money in their possession when they were arrested, making up just a small part of the $4,000 or $5,000 they had stolen. One of them started to draw his pistol, but X. got the drop on him.[85]

FOOLED BY JOE KIPP

Al Wilkins told a story about Joe Kipp trading whiskey among the Indians and fooling X. Beidler along the way.

> *When my father and I came into Montana from the Canadian northwest in 1873, we found the people much different from any we had known in the states, east or south. It was the custom in western territories for men to look after each other's interests, and for the first time we learned the real meaning of the old saying, "A friend in need is a friend indeed."*
>
> *By the winter of 1874–75 we were located at a trading post on the Marias River. Joe Kipp, a half-breed Indian, spent the winter with us, and we found him to be a man of unusual personality. He told us his father had been one of the managers for the old Hudson's Bay Fur company. His father sent Joe to school at St. Louis and gave him a college education. Joe was more white than Indian, with light brown hair and rather light eyes. He was a great Indian trader and often supplied them with whiskey.*
>
> *I remember an incident in the spring of 1875, when I was hunting on Teton river four miles back of Fort Benton. I noticed a wagon coming down one of the ridges as fast as the team could run and a mile further back another wagon was coming pell-mell on the same trail. I headed for the river, where I thought the first team would strike it, to see what was up. When I reached the river Joe Kipp had driven into it and thrown 10 kegs of whisky into the stream. Joe had just time to dump the whisky, drive across the river and begin unhitching his horses when X. Beidler came rushing up.*

Biracial Indian trader Joe Kipp lived life on the edge, between Native and White worlds. Photo by Charles S. Francis. *Author's collection.*

PULLED A FAST ONE

"No use unhitching, Joe," X. began, "I know you started out with whisky to trade with the Indians, and it is my duty as United States marshal to put a stop to that business."

"Well," Joe said, "stop it, then, I have no objections. Search my outfit, if you want to, but you haven't got anything on me."

X. searched Kipp's wagon and found nothing in it except a few Indian trinkets and trade goods. He turned to me and asked me what Kipp had done with the whisky. I told that if Kipp had brought any whisky into camp I hadn't seen it. Then Beidler asked Kipp what he was running so for if he didn't have any contraband stuff in his wagon, and Kipp said that when he saw Beidler after him he thought it was a holdup and was mighty glad when he saw it was only X. Beidler behind him.

"It's dinner time," Kipp said, "so you fellows turn your donkeys loose to graze, and we'll have a mulligan before you go back." I had an antelope on the back of my saddle, so I furnished the meat and Kipp furnished the bacon to fry it with and crackers and tea. X. did full justice to the feed, saying it sure tasted good after the race over the rough prairie. After dinner we all had a smoke at X.'s expense, and he hooked up and left for the post.

I was curious to find whether Kipp would recover any of his whisky and waited to see.

WHISKY FOUND

After the marshal disappeared, Kipp said, "There is a riffle just around the bend, where we will likely find most of the kegs." Sure enough, there was all the whisky lined up in shallow water, every keg Kipp dumped overboard. "This stuff will all be traded for robes and furs tonight," Kipp said, "and tomorrow night I'll be back at the fort again." The next afternoon Kipp drove in with a fine lot of furs.[86]

ARRESTING CYPRESS HILLS SUSPECTS

At Fort Benton on June 21, 1875, John H. Evans, age twenty-nine, of Fort Dodge, Iowa; Trevanion Hale, thirty-five, Glenwood, Iowa; Samuel A. Harper, twenty-seven, Coshocton, Ohio; Thomas W. Hardwick, thirty-two, Carrollton, Missouri; and Elijah John Devereaux, forty, Maine, were arrested by Deputy Marshals X. Beidler and Charles Hard, assisted by local 7th Infantry soldiers, for killing Nakota Indians at the Cypress Hills "Massacre" in May 1873. The warrant for the arrest of the men was issued at the insistence of the British government through a special commissioner, W.E. Cullan, appointed to investigate the matter. The extradition trial followed in Helena, raising intense passions throughout Montana Territory and leading to the release of the prisoners for lack of evidence, followed by their triumphant return to Fort Benton and the opening of the Extradition Saloon in their honor.[87]

BEIDLER ON THE WARPATH

In January 1876, Pend D'Oreille raided twenty horses from the Gros Ventres camp twenty miles below Fort Benton. That tribe complained to Deputy Marshal Beidler and asked for their recovery. The *Benton Record* reported this unusual development whereby a tribe appealed for help rather than waging their own counter horse raid:

The Gros Ventres being at peace with all the neighboring tribes and acting well throughout, Marshal Beidler promised to recover their property for them. The Pend D'Oreille were then camped on the Teton river north of Fort Shaw.

The Marshal went to the commandant of the military post [Colonel John Gibbon] *and stated the case, when that officer sent for the Indians and ordered them to deliver up the stolen horses or return others in their place.*

This they did as far as they were able, but the Marshal was not satisfied; and with the assistance of the military, he proceeded to the main camp and recovered the remainder of the stolen property.

Marshal Beidler arrived at Benton on Monday, accompanied by [a Gros Ventre] *Indian, with the horses in his possession, which were immediately turned over to their proper owners. This is the first instance of the kind, and its good effect upon the Indians is incalculable.*[88]

In April 1876, Marshal Beidler, assisted by Lieutenant Harding and a military escort, captured fifteen gallons of alcohol on the Marias River.[89] In early June, Beidler arrived at Fort Benton on the steamboat

Woodhawks lived along the Missouri River, in a dangerous and lawless environment, supplying the vital wood to fuel steamboats. *Author's collection.*

A cabin register records that "J.H. Beadler" (J.X. Beidler) and his unidentified prisoner boarded the steamboat *Butte* at Carroll en route to Fort Benton, arriving on July 13, 1881. Also boarding at Carroll were Choteau County sheriff Johnny Healy and Joe Kipp. *OHRC.*

Western. X. boarded at Fort Peck with a prisoner, Samuel Bosler, whom he had captured at Tom How's woodyard, fifteen miles below the mouth of Milk River.[90]

A LAWMAN OF MANY DIMENSIONS

X. Beidler ranged widely from his Fort Benton headquarters over the years of the early 1880s. He sought, arrested and transported criminals as diverse as the fascinating Blackfoot Spopee (the Turtle) and other murderers to army deserters, horse capturers, smugglers and thieves of many kinds— and always had a story to tell. Truly, in the words of Montana's first U.S. senator, Wilbur Fisk Sanders, X. Beidler "brought more law and order to the Montana frontier than any other pioneer."[91]

Chapter 11

THE GREATEST SOCIAL EVENT

Opening the Grandest Hotel

*T*he Grand Union Hotel opened on November 2, 1882, featuring the greatest social event in Fort Benton's early history. People came from all over the broad trading area. English members of Parliament and North West Mounted Police came down from Canada. Wolfers abandoned their traps and strychnine. Wagon masters held up their ox trains, with drivers, mule skinners, bullwhackers and roustabouts coming to celebrate. Miners came from their diggings, and stockmen and cowboys left their ranches—Charlie Russell reportedly came over from the Judith River Country. Remarkably, nearly one hundred White ladies from Fort Benton and the surrounding towns and ranches joined in the celebration—a decade earlier, White women could have been counted on one hand.[92]

The Grand Union was built in Victorian style and furnished at a cost of $200,000 (almost $6 million today). Five hundred thousand bricks, all made at Fort Benton, went into its construction. It was designed by architect Thomas Tweedy, who supervised construction until one month before opening, when the owners hired master carpenter Whitman Gibson "W.G." Jones and his men to complete the interior carpentry work with painters Keenan & Payne. Tweedy objected and, in a huff, resigned as superintendent. Jones completed the interior work and, the next summer, added a fine porch to the front entrance of the hotel.[93] The *Benton Record* reported the grand opening in style.

Grand Union Hotel,

FORT BENTON, M. T.

The Leading Hotel of Montana Territory.

First-Class in all of its Appointments.

THE FINEST and LARGEST

hotel building in the West. Opened November 2, 1882.

—o—

First-Class Accommodations for the Traveling Public. Sample Rooms for Commercial Travelers.

This house is centrally located, and all coaches arrive at and depart from the door. First-class Bar and Billiard Room in the house. Charges reasonable.

—o—

STEPHEN SPITZLEY & CO., Propr's.

Above: The Grand Union Hotel in 1883 during the last great years of the steamboat trade. *OHRC*.

Left: First advertising for the Grand Union, the "Leading hotel of Montana." River Press, *December 6, 1882.*

An Opening to Remember

GRAND OPENING: The Grand Union Hotel of Benton
Ball and supper—Description of the Building...

The grandest affair of its kind ever witnessed in Benton, and most probably in the Territory, was the opening ball of the largest hotel in Montana, the Grand Union of Benton, by Messrs. Stephen Spitzley & Co., last evening. For some time past the proprietors have been busily engaged in preparing for the coming ball which took place last night, and the number of lives of chickens, turkeys, ducks, and geese which Mr. A.A. Martin, chief cook, and his able corps of culinary assistants, will have to answer for is perfectly overwhelming. The affair commenced by using the following invitation:

GRAND OPENING

Yourself and ladies are respectfully invited to attend the opening ball at the Grand Union Hotel, Fort Benton, Montana, Thursday, November, 2d, 1882. Tickets with supper, $3.00....

The social world was on the tiptoe of expectation. About 8:30 p.m. the guests began to assemble and before 9:30 between 200 and 300 guests had arrived and were in the different dressing rooms and the hotel dining which was used for the dancing hall for the evening, on the river side of which was erected a raised platform about three feet high and upon which were the members of the Benton String Band, together with Mr. Claus Peters, who furnished the music for the occasion. The dancing commenced soon after the arrival of the guests in the dining room, which was admirably adapted for the purpose for which it was used....

THE DANCING

There were [many] *ladies present, and the floor had eight to twelve sets dancing quadrilles at the same time, and all seemed to enjoy themselves immensely.* [A dozen dance sets ranging from quadrilles to waltzes to polkas continued before supper, and another dozen resumed after the feast.]

THE LADIES

The ladies as they always do, looked beautifully, and a great many of them were very tastefully dressed....

SUPPER

The supper was announced at 12 o'clock and was a grand affair and did credit not only to Messrs. Stephen Spitzley & Co., but also to Messrs. Martin, Flowers and Jones, the cooks. The bill of fare was as follows:

MENU:
Lobster Salad, Chicken Salad.
Loin of Beef, Haunch of Mutton,
Spring Chicken, Boned Turkey,
Spiced Beef, Ox Tongue,
Boned Leg of Veal.
FRUITS:
Green Apples, Nuts, Macedoine Fruits,
Charlotte Russe, Ice Cream,
Assorted Cake.

The dancing was kept up until a very late hour, when the assembled guests retired to their homes delighted with the festivities of the occasion, and at having been present at the grandest affair of its kind ever witnessed in Benton, and with the pleasant manner in which they had been entertained....

DESCRIPTION OF THE HOTEL

An account of the grand opening would be incomplete without a description of the hotel itself. It is about 115 feet long and 85 feet wide, and is built of brick, three stories high. It faces down the river, with the Missouri river on the right, and Front Street on its left, and has a plank sidewalk on its front and left sides about twelve feet wide. The following are the names of the employes of the Grand Union Hotel:

W.H. Todd, clerk; Mrs. A.L. Marsten, housekeeper; Edward S. Smith, barkeeper; Lafayette Hall, poster; Alex. A. Martin, chief cook; J. Flowers, second cook; Samuel Jones, third cook; Henry Courtney, head waiter; Frank Martin, waiter; Charles Carroll, waiter, and Mrs. Henrietta Johnson, chambermaid. [All but the first three were African American.]

THE OFFICE

The office is under the superintendence of Mr. W.H. Todd, who officiates behind one of the finest hotel counters in Montana, which was made by Messrs. Jones & Merrill, of Benton. It is 16 feet long on its

The popular saloon at the Grand Union featured a special back bar built by Butte master carpenter Charles Merrill. The back bar now resides at the Shack in Missoula. *OHRC.*

longest side, and then curves back six feet, and upon it is stained glass set in a frame, and an aperture through which the clerk can see all that is going on and receive payments....

THE BAR ROOM

is on the northwest corner of the whole building, and in a room which is about 20x25 feet, and which has just been furnished, and is kept by Mr. Edward S. Smith. [Within weeks of opening, a fine bar, designed and built by Charles Merrill, was installed in the bar room.]

WASHROOM

Immediately in the rear of the office is the washroom, 12x18 feet, containing six marble basins, and just behind them is a heavy zinc tank about three feet high for supplying the water used in the basins, and which is done by faucets. Underneath the basins is a sink and sewer, which connects with the Missouri river about 100 feet from the building, for the purpose of draining the waste water.

THE DINING ROOM

is 30x60 feet. The residents of Benton have visited it so much as to scarcely require any description. There are six dining tables, three of which are extension tablets, and the others are ordinary tables. The ordinary ones are 6x3 feet....

THE KITCHEN

is not yet fitted up or completed, but it contains a large Charter Oak range, made by G.W. Filley, St. Louis, Mo., and we understand there is to be a still larger and finer range to be put up next spring...

LADIES' PARLORS

There are two ladies' parlors both of the same size, 35x20 feet. These rooms are connected by folding doors but are not yet furnished. The rooms are finely located, one above the office and the other on the northwest corner of the building, and each room is lighted up by three windows which command a complete view of the town, especially the levee and the Missouri river as far as the promontory below town.

THE BRIDAL CHAMBER

The bridal chamber is adjoining the ladies' parlor, with which it communicates by a door, and is not yet quite fitted up. The carpet is laid, and in the room is a bureau, washstand, together with a bedstead costing $200.

THE LADIES' ENTRANCE

The ladies' entrance is on the west side of the building and has a large double door opening into a hall in which is the stairway connecting it with the upper floor and the ladies' parlor. To the right of the ladies' entrance is the barber shop of Messrs. Bryar & Anderson, who are too well known to require more than a mere mention.

BED ROOMS

There are 60 bedrooms for guests in the house, amongst which are six suites of rooms for families with folding doors.[94]

THE JEWEL IN FORT BENTON'S CROWN: A HISTORY

Grand Union Hotel's 140th Anniversary, November 1, 1882–November 1, 2022

The Grand Union Hotel is both the oldest operating hotel and among the most important historic buildings in Montana. Completed in 1882 at the height of the steamboat era on the Upper Missouri, the Grand Union welcomed weary travelers to spend a few nights in its luxury before they set out to less "refined places" like Virginia City and points west.

The architectural character of the Grand Union was unique, with bricks carefully fitted into excellent bold decorations. Its extensive corbelling, wrought iron balconies and ornate chimneys were an impressive sight. The dining room was furnished with Victorian appointments, and its silver service, white linen and Bavarian china served the rich and famous. An elegant ladies' parlor on the second floor, with a private stairway to the dining room, saved the ladies from exposure to the raucous crowd in the saloon and poker rooms. The ornate lobby desk and broad black walnut staircase highlighted the fine carpentry work throughout. No wonder that the opening ball for the Grand Union was the grandest affair ever witnessed in Benton—and perhaps in Montana Territory.

The Grand Union, during its 140 years, has had many lives: the most luxurious hotel between St. Louis and Seattle; a run-of-the-mill hotel; a virtual flophouse with rooms to rent for two bits; and years of derelict closure. But James and Cheryl Gagnon brought the grand old lady of Montana hotels back in the 1990s, brightly restored to its golden-era glory with shining modernity carefully folded in. This is the story of the jewel in Fort Benton's crown.

At the height of the steamboat era in 1879, William H. Todd had a dream. Fort Benton was booming, with thousands of passengers and many tons of freight arriving at the head of navigation on the Upper Missouri. With trails leading in every direction, Fort Benton was the transportation hub of bustling Montana Territory. Billy Todd bought lot one, block one, on the steamboat levee, forty-two feet of which fronted on Front Street and one hundred on Bond Street (now Fourteenth).

The next year, 1880, Todd talked constantly about a grand hotel positioned to receive travelers as they stepped off the steamboats to afford them a day or two of luxury before they set out by horseback, stage or wagon to the Canadian frontier or the many mining towns in Montana

Territory. Billy Todd convinced the optimistic businessmen of Fort Benton that the town was a refined, permanent community with a great future. By September 1880, a corporation had been formed to raise money for the Benton Hotel Company. Within a month, the contract was let to Storer and Storer to furnish locally made bricks. Cold weather arrived in November, closing out the booming building season before most of the bricks could be manufactured, and Fort Benton went into its winter slumber.

In the spring of 1881, just as the weather warmed enough to permit resumption of brickmaking and construction work, the brickmakers dissolved their partnership, and rumors began to fly that the new hotel would never be built. But Todd and his supporters were determined to press forward. In August, ground was broken for the hotel, with Todd in general charge of construction and Thomas Tweedy as architect and superintendent of construction. Legend has it that the hotel had no architect; rather, the craftsmen simply designed it as they built. Yet apparently the first elaborate plans were drawn up by an unknown eastern architect and then either downsized or ignored by Tweedy.

Plans jelled by August 1881 for a three-story brick hotel, seventy-five feet, four inches on Front Street by eighty feet, four inches on Bond Street. The principal entrance was to be on Bond Street and the ladies' entrance on Front. The main entrance would lead into a lobby with a grand staircase ascending to the second floor. The dining room would front on the river, while the room at the corner of Front and Bond would serve as a saloon and billiard hall. The south room on Front Street could be rented for a barbershop. Just over one year later, these plans came true.

By the end of August 1881, the Square Butte quarry Shonkinite granite foundation was in place and the first bricks laid, with Frank Coombs, a local contractor, supervising the brickwork, which would eventually total half a million bricks. Tweedy insisted on the best-seasoned wood for floor joists, and the project suffered delays in the supply of lumber. Meanwhile, Benton's other hotels, the Choteau House, the Overland and the Centennial, were doing booming business. Building costs were escalating in the river city.

After slowing for the winter, construction on the new, as-yet-unnamed hotel accelerated in the spring of 1882. The arrival of the steamboat *Josephine* on May 3 signaled the opening of another great year at the head of navigation. Boats began to arrive almost daily, loaded with travelers and cargo for the territory and fine furnishings for the new hotel. The steamer *Helena* brought carpet, stoves and a grand piano. The *Benton* arrived with more carpeting and ceiling and flooring materials. The *Butte* brought chairs and glassware for the new hotel. The *Helena*, on its second trip, brought walnut boards destined to be assembled into the hotel's grand staircase.

In June, plastering began, and a few days later, the steamer *Black Hills* arrived with the doors and windows, tailor-made in Anoka, Minnesota. *Benton*'s second trip brought sofas, settees, ladies' desks, boxes of marble dressers, beds and bureaus from Duluth. The hotel's famous safe arrived in July on the *Benton*'s third trip from Bismarck. As the summer passed and the water level lowered, boats had to land at Coal Banks, like the *Butte* with its cargo of seventy barrels of china destined to grace the tables of the fine dining room in the new hotel.

The name, Grand Union, was finally announced in the *River Press* on September 27, 1882. The two words, *grand* and *union*, fit the post–Civil War times and the glorious Union victory. The Grand Union was the perfect name for the finest hotel in the West. During furious activity to complete construction, decorate the interior and hire a staff, Tweedy angrily resigned, and W.G. Jones, a master carpenter, completed the carpentry work, which was running behind schedule. Finally, the interior work was almost complete, and the hotel was ready to open.

Bentonites got their first look inside the Grand Union Hotel on Thursday, November 2, 1882. That evening, the grand affair was held, a spectacular opening ball worthy of the fine new hotel. An elaborate program unfolded over the course of the evening, with dancing showing one hundred ladies in their finest. At midnight, a supper feast was served, prepared by Benton's finest chef, young Black Alex Martin. Reflecting the robust Black community in Fort Benton at the time, the entire staff of eleven at the new hotel was African American, except three supervisors.

The ball continued with more dancing until the wee hours of the morning. The *Benton Record* dedicated much of its next edition to describing the grand ball and the new hotel in elaborate detail. The proudest man on the scene must have been Billy Todd, who, after years of dreaming and fifteen months of construction, at last was standing in the lobby of the Grand Union contemplating the great future of the hotel and Fort Benton.

The first guest at the Grand Union was Alex Staveley Hill, a British capitalist and member of Parliament. Another ninety-plus guests packed the small rooms that first night, including Hill's brother; Fort Benton's most prominent citizens, like the Conrad family, T.E. Collins, Hans Wackerlin, W.S. Wetzel, W.S. Stocking and Paris Gibson; and prominent visitors from San Francisco, Ottawa, Pittsburgh, New York City and St. Louis.

Since it was unladylike for a woman to walk through the men's world of the lobby and saloon, the Grand Union had a ladies' side door. A lady would enter the hotel by that door and climb a staircase up to the women's parlor on the second floor. When nature called, guests would go out the back door of the hotel across a catwalk to a remarkable two-story-high, sixteen-hole outhouse.

The men's saloon was a lively place, especially when the many cattlemen and cowboys in the area came to town. Drinking and gambling sometimes led to the birth of legends, such as the time when two cowboys bet on whether one could ride his horse all the way up the lobby staircase. The bet was made, and the cowboy went out to the street to untie his horse. He led the horse through the front doors, mounted and made it up to the first landing before the night clerk heard the commotion and acted. The outcome of the bet was settled when the clerk shot the rider. So goes the legend.

The dawn of the New Year 1883 brought another booming navigation season, but the end was near for steamboating. The Utah Northern Railroad had long since opened the railroad era in Montana, and late 1883 brought the Northern Pacific into Helena. Equally threateningly, the Canadian Pacific railroad arrived in Alberta in 1883. The next year, sheep rancher Paris Gibson began building the town of Great Falls above the falls of the Missouri. James J. Hill's Manitoba Railroad arrived in the fall of 1887. The days of Fort Benton as a transportation hub both north and south of the Medicine Line were ending, and Fort Benton's population began to plunge. Shocking evidence of this came in 1884 when the Benton Hotel Company assets went at a sheriff's sale to a banking firm.

The challenge for a series of hotelmen in Fort Benton over the next two decades then became how to keep the magnificent Grand Union operating and make it pay. In 1899, local businessmen J.H. Green and B.F. O'Neal bought the hotel for $10,000. Major remodeling took place about 1900, and in 1917, Mr. and Mrs. Charles Lepley took on the challenge.

While river traffic had ended, and Great Falls and Lethbridge were now transportation hubs, Fort Benton began to come back, riding the good years of open-range cattle ranching and, in the early 1900s, an amazing homesteading boom. Fort Benton settled into a long era as the agricultural center of Montana's Golden Triangle, with the good and bad years that come with widely varying weather and commodity prices.

During the 1930s and '40s, the Grand Union went steadily downhill. The bedrooms, once among the best in the West, gained a reputation for having

This outrageous scene of a cowboy riding his horse up the grand staircase at the Grand Union illustrates one of the many tales of this grand hotel. *Author's collection.*

a permanent insect population exceeded only by that of the disreputable Choteau House. Stories made the rounds about time spent at the not-so-grand Union:

> *I had just climbed into one of the only creaking brass beds and was beginning to get drowsy when I heard some weak voices singing. I couldn't make out the words at first, but by holding my breath they came clearer. It seemed to be two men. I listened carefully in the silence.*

Above: The Grand Union's 125th anniversary was served in style with special events and a special edition of the *River Press*. *Author's collection.*

Opposite: Former co-owner and manager Cheryl Gagnon (*center*) and her husband, James, saved and restored the Grand Union, bringing it back to its glory days as the jewel in the crown of Fort Benton. *Author's photo.*

"Pull for the shore, boys, pull for the shore."

Was it a ghost? A group of drowned crewmen from one of the steamboats? Again, it came:

"Pull for the shore, boys, pull for the shore."

Though the voices were weak, they seemed to come from right under the bed. Getting my flashlight, I looked under. There in the pot were two bedbugs on a matchstick singing:

"Pull for the shore, boys, pull for the shore."[95]

Charles Lepley died in 1941, and his wife, May, took over operation for another decade, then sold the hotel to Harold Thomas and his wife, Margaretha, the legendary superintendent of Chouteau County schools.

By this time, little "grand" remained in the hotel in the eyes of Harold Thomas:

The lobby, dining room, and saloon were ghosts of a once elegant era. Rooms were threadbare with straw mattresses still sprawling on sagging springs. Two public bathrooms on each of the three floors were the only personal sanitary facilities....

The Grand Union continues operation today as one of Montana's oldest and finest hotels. *Author's photo.*

One day shortly after we moved in a friend of mine asked me how in the hell I ever got into this mess. The only answer I've been able to find is that the building offered a challenge to a restless soul and a stubborn nature.[96]

The one-man restoration effort of Harold Thomas likely saved the structure, which by then was on the National Register of Historic Places. Over a quarter century, Thomas removed the colorful but dangerous chimneys, sealed holes, repaired cornices, painted, added structural supports, put in new plumbing and wiring and fumigated. In 1979, Mr. and Mrs. Thomas sold the hotel to Levee Restorations. Despite good intentions, they never raised the funds needed to bring the hotel back into operation.

The Grand Union, over many years, had many lives, ending in derelict closure. But in the 1990s, James and Cheryl Gagnon brought the grand old lady back, brightly restored to its golden-era glory with shining modernity embedded in. Fort Benton's crown jewel shines brightly today under new owners Tony and Colette Longin.[97]

Chapter 12

LET THERE BE LIGHT

The Rose Bud *Lights Up the Night*

T he steamboat *Rose Bud* departed Bismarck on July 4, 1882, with 247 tons of cargo and five passengers. Above Fort Union, it loaded twenty-seven more passengers from the sunken *Red Cloud*. The *Rose Bud* arrived at Fort Benton on July 19 to deliver the passengers and freight— and to demonstrate for the first time electricity as a wondrous source of light.

The *Rose Bud*, build in 1877 at the California yard on the Monongahela River in Pennsylvania for the Coulson line, made more than fifty trips to Fort Benton. It set a record as the first boat to arrive at Fort Benton in four different years. Yet it would be this 1882 trip that would become *Rose Bud*'s most memorable.[98]

A large crowd gathered at the levee when darkness fell, late that summer evening. The crude steam generator was started and furnished electricity to power a floodlight, which directed a beam over Fort Benton. The light beam played on the tallest and grandest building in town, the Grand Union, to show its power and the distance it would carry. As the spotlight lighted a balcony of the hotel, it brought into view a prominent bachelor of the town, amorously entwined with the wife of a leading citizen. This was a shock that had not been anticipated.

The *River Press* reported this exciting electrical development:

THE ELECTRIC LIGHT

The Rose Bud *steamed up last evening and gave an exhibition of the working of the electric light for the benefit of our citizens. Nearly everybody*

The *Rose Bud* brought the first electric lights to the Upper Missouri. Here, *Rose Bud*, with an electric light visible, is at Judith Landing with passengers including North West Mounted Police in helmets ashore. *OHRC.*

was out to see it, and on all hands, it was pronounced a great success for the purpose designed—navigating the Big Muddy on dark nights—while at the same time the fact was made manifest that the light can be successfully employed for street illuminating purposes.

The Rose Bud *is the first Missouri river boat to test the electric light, and the officers throughout pronounce it a great success. It is estimated that from two to three days' time can be saved on a trip from Bismarck up using the light, which enables the boat to run the darkest nights with perfect safety, while without it she would be compelled to tie up and wait for daylight.*

The electric light is in general use on the Mississippi and Ohio rivers, and there is no good reason why the boats on the Upper Missouri should not have it as well. In the case of the Rose Bud, *it is an experiment, and as it has proved so great a success it is probable that every boat on the river will have the light next season. Once the plant is secured, there is but very little expense attached to operating it. The motive power is already at hand and the cost of the carbons—about twenty cents a night—is the only expense*

Steamboat *Rose Bud* underway at Deadman's Rapids on the Upper Missouri. *OHRC.*

additional. There are two lights, one with a large reflector which is used when the boat is in motion, and it illuminates the river perfectly nearly a mile ahead; the other has no reflector, and is employed to light up around the boat when loading wood, etc. The change from one light to the other can be made readily and instantly. The light is not as powerful as those used for illuminating cities, but it is all that is needed. Those who witnessed the illumination last evening agree with the officers of the boat that it is a grand success, and we trust next season will come into general use on the upper Big Muddy.[99]

The steamboat *Helena* wooding at night, with a big bonfire for light. With electric lights, steamboats could operate at night with no bonfires needed for wooding. *Painting by artist J.E. Trott, in author's collection. Courtesy of Peter C. Trott.*

A select few comprehended the significance of the demonstration. Town boosters seized the scene to pronounce that Benton was ahead as usual, being the first town in Montana Territory to have the electric light.

However, did this happen? Weeks earlier, at Bismarck, Dakota Territory, E.H. Thompson, an electrician from St. Paul, had mounted electric lights on the *Rose Bud* at a cost of about $1,500. At a woodyard on the way up the river, the light was turned on in full force on the wood stacked up, and the frightened woodhawk sought a hiding place from which he could not be induced to emerge to negotiate with the clerk of the boat for the sale of his stock on hand. He, however, did venture to hold up his hand with three fingers unflexed, to indicate that three dollars per cord would take the load.[100]

Remarkably, less than three years earlier, on December 31, 1879, Thomas Edison first publicly demonstrated his electric incandescent light by illuminating some forty bulbs at his laboratory in Menlo Park, New Jersey. In November 1879, Edison filed to acquire a U.S. patent for an electric lamp using a carbon filament or strip coiled and connected to platina contact wires. The patent came through in January 1880, but by that time, Edison had put hours of tests and research into perfecting the electric bulb. Three years later, the overhead electric lighting system designed by Thomas Edison for Roselle, New Jersey, was used for the first time, making it the first city in the world to be lit up by electricity.[101]

Edison's remarkable invention changed the way the world lived and functioned. And in mid-1882, the steamboat *Rose Bud* was demonstrating electric lights in Fort Benton. By the end of 1882, both Helena and Butte had begun to illuminate their cities with electric lights. Ironically, the arrival of electricity would destroy any chance Fort Benton had of becoming the industrial giant in northern Montana. The falls of the Missouri, just thirty miles upstream, which had brought such great success to Fort Benton as the head of river navigation, would now ensure that it would never be more than the county seat of an agricultural community. When the falls of the Missouri were harnessed to produce power, industry built up rapidly in the 1890s in the "future great," the new city of Great Falls, not in Fort Benton.[102]

Chapter 13

THE MONTANA YEARS OF THE GANDHI OF THE MÉTIS

Louis Riel in Exile

No figure in western Canadian history is more controversial than the eloquent, brilliant, mystical Métis leader Louis Riel—and Fort Benton shares his powerful tale. A hero to his people and French Canadians, a villain to many English Canadians, Louis Riel spent five years from 1879 to 1884 in exile in Montana centered on Fort Benton before his death by hanging for leading the Red River Rebellion of 1885.

Riel was earlier exiled for leading the Red River Resistance in 1869–70. In the last year of his exile, in 1879, Riel and many of the Métis moved to the valleys of the Upper Missouri of Montana Territory to hunt the increasingly scarce buffalo. There, he became a trader and interpreter as his people wandered the turbulent Montana frontier, demoralized and enduring economic hardship. As Riel observed the effects of alcohol and the problems of his people, he became a forceful activist in Montana politics as he tried to suppress the alcohol trade and create a "reserve" for the Métis in northern Montana.

MEETING LOUIS RIEL

Perhaps the best introduction to the remarkable Louis Riel is reading Martha Edgerton Rolfe's description of her first meeting with the great Métis leader during the years that she and Herbert Percy lived in Fort Benton. The daughter of Montana's first territorial governor, Sidney Edgerton, Martha's knowledge of Montana pioneers was unsurpassed.

One evening at sunset in the summer of 1883, someone knocked at the door of our house in Fort Benton, situated on the hill above town, and near the stage road. I opened the door to find a man standing there dressed like a hunter, or possibly a rancher. He inquired if my husband was at home. I told him "No, but I expect him any minute," and added "Will you come in and wait for him?" He accepted the invitation and entered the house.

As there was no hat rack, I offered to take his cap, which he had removed on entering; an act of courtesy uncommon on the part of frontiersmen in those days, who seemed to feel that a roof was not adequate protection for the head. The man hesitatingly extended his cap to me, remarking as he did so, "Ah, Madam, it is too poor." At this I looked at him more intently, thinking as I did so, "This man is well bred."

After exile in Montana Territory, visionary Métis leader Louis Riel returned to Canada to lead the 1885 Red River Rebellion. *Author's collection.*

I saw that he was of medium height, light complexioned, with hair of a reddish color, according to my recollection—many years have passed since then—blue eyes. His nose was his most pronounced feature, being of good length, and aquiline—the nose of the leader.

He was scarcely seated before Mr. Rolfe arrived, and at once introduced the stranger as "Louis Riel." The name meant nothing to me, except that it had a foreign sound, and I thought him to be a Frenchman. He was in some difficulty with the authorities at Fort Benton, and Mr. Rolfe acted as his attorney. After discussion of business, the conversation turned to other subjects, and for a couple of hours, Riel held us spellbound by the narration of his experiences in Montana. He had a wonderful voice for speaking, strong, and with a resonance I never heard equalized. He, like Leon Trotsky, evidently had the ability to make himself heard at a great distance in the open air.

At one town where he and his people were encamped, one of the county officials, without the slightest show of legality, charged into their midst and drove off their finest horses to add to his own large band. His people were helpless; it was useless for them to appeal to the authorities; they were "Breeds," with no rights a White man was bound to respect. All they could do was to submit in silence to the outrage. This was but one of the many stories he narrated, that led me to see how such treatment will react on a sensitive nature, such as Louis Riel possessed from his Gallic inheritance, if not from his Irish forebears, who were undoubtedly as quick to resent an injury, as were his Indian ancestors.

Louis Riel, who was born near Fort Garry, now Winnipeg, in 1844, was the son of Louis Riel and Julie de Lagimonière and had very little Indian blood. It has been said that the Crees of today, are many of them descendants of the noblest families in France. The prefix to his mother's name, would indicate that she, who was but part Indian, was one of these.

The elder Louis Riel, known as the "Miller of the Seine," was undoubtedly a man of considerable force of character, and a recognized leader. Once, when trouble had arisen between the French and Half-breed settlers and the authorities, the elder Riel was called upon to lead the opposition and was victorious.

Louis Riel the Second must, from his earliest years, have gained recognition as being more than ordinarily intelligent, as he became an archbishop's protegee, who gave him a college education, to fit him for the priesthood. The first so-called, "Rebellion," in which he took part, occurred [in 1869–70] when the Hudson's Bay company sold their lands in Manitoba to the new Dominion Government, without the consent of the settlers, who, according to Catholic writers, were at least half of them French Half-breeds.

The rising was not intended as a rebellion, but as an organized protest against the action of the government, which they held was illegal. These people had laid their grievances before the Ottawa officials with no result. Their petitions proving ineffective, they tried what virtue there was in bullets. They turned back the Dominion Governor at the American boundary line, and held the country for ten months, Colonel, later General [Garnet Joseph] Wolseley, was sent with a body of troops to put down the insurrection. It could not pass through the United States, as it was a military expedition, and therefore had to make its way through the unbroken forests north of the Boundary, which was an additional grievance to be laid to the charge of the rebels.

During the rising, an Orangeman, named Scott, who expressed his opposition to some of the leader's acts, was arrested and shot. I can find no evidence that Riel was his executor, although he is charged with this so-called murder, which was committed after Scott's trial by court martial and the death sentence pronounced against him. However that may be, the leaders, and those who took part in the rising were rigorously dealt with at the time of its suppression. Riel was outlawed, and money *offered by the Ottawa government for his apprehension. His defeat, and his efforts to elude his pursuers, resulted in his becoming temporarily insane, when he was confined in various asylums. On his recovery— if he ever fully recovered—he gave valuable aid to the government during the Fenian agitation, that won for him the commendation of the Lieutenant-Governor.*

Riel was twice elected to the Dominion Parliament. The first time he did not appear to take his seat, and on the second occasion he was debarred from doing so.

Being, in effect, exiled from Canada, he became a citizen of the United States, and was living in Montana.[103]

In September 1879, Louis Riel left the St. Joseph-Pembina community, arriving in Montana Territory and wintering among the Métis on Flat Willow Creek, a tributary of the Musselshell River.[104] The *Benton Record* first announced Riel's presence in Montana in December 1879, reporting: "Reel [*sic*], the noted leader of the Northern Half-Breeds, is said to be at, or near, Fort Assinniboine, awaiting the termination of his exile."[105]

In 1880, Riel's "Montana agenda" became clear when he filed for citizenship and petitioned for a Métis reserve. On May 17, he filed a Declaration of Intent for U.S. Citizenship with the clerk of court in Fort Benton.[106]

On August 6, from a camp on the Musselshell River, Riel wrote a letter to "Brevet Major General" N.A. Miles, asking him to forward to the proper authorities in the U.S. government a petition, signed by eighty-one Métis, asking for "a portion of land as a special reservation for the halfbreeds" in northern Montana Territory. Funds were requested for schools, agricultural equipment and seeds and livestock for the Métis to settle and own land through the Homestead Act or other legislation. In return, the petition promised that the Métis would "live as law abiding people."[107]

Later in August, Riel and fifty Métis followers visited Miles City seeking a location for settlement. A month later, "Louis Reil [*sic*], the Manitoba patriot, was back in Fort Benton purchasing supplies for the fall and winter prairie trade."[108]

In Pointe-au-Loup, Fort Berthold, Dakota Territory, in the spring of 1881, Riel married young Métis Marguerite Monet *dite* Bellehumeur according to the custom of the country (*la manner du pays*) on April 28, the marriage being solemnized on March 9, 1882.[109]

Of modest means and perennially short of money, in March 1882, Riel set aside his political activities to gain employment. With Marguerite, he drove his Red River cart to the extensive sheep ranch of Civil War veteran Henry "Mac" MacDonald, nestled in the eastern foothills of the Highwood Mountains, south of Fort Benton. Mac was working at the home corral when he heard the distinctive sound of the cart approaching, and he described its arrival:

> *A man sprang lightly from the wagon. He came forward elaborately sweeping his broad-brimmed black hat before him and bowing deeply from the waist in the manner of the old French courtiers.*
>
> *"Good day, M'sieur," was his greeting.*
>
> *His modulated, resonant voice surprised Mac, for the fellow was obviously wilderness-born, a man above medium height, slim and sinewy as a panther. Shaggy locks of reddish-brown hair clipped just above the shoulders, framed his bearded face. His eyes shone with a wild brilliance but, because his glance shifted constantly, it was impossible to tell whether they were brown or very dark blue. His nose was strongly aquiline, and his skin was tanned. However, nothing about his features suggested the Indian, except his high cheekbones. He wore the black clothing and red sash characteristic of the Red River breeds. With a feeling that he had seen this man before, Henry answered his greeting reservedly.*
>
> *"M'sieur," said the newcomer. "My name is Riel—Louis David Riel. I do not flatter myself that to a busy man like you the poor name means anything."*
>
> *It did mean something. Mac recalled now who he was, and a little of his history. He went over it rapidly in his mind while the half-breed stood before him, smiling ingratiatingly.*[110]

Mac recalled hearing in Fort Benton about Riel and his Manitoban Métis "half-breeds," descendants of the French Canadian voyageurs, rising up in an armed protest on the transfer of the Hudson's Bay Company's territory to the newly established Dominion of Canada, only to have their insurgency put down after some initial successes, ending in a sentence of exile from the dominion.

After a long conversation, Mac hired Riel. Over the next several months, Mac kept Riel working close to his ranch, concerned about his ability to herd sheep. Finally, Riel convinced Mac to assign a herd to him. It quickly became apparent to Mac that Riel was not suited for the job, constantly "losing" his flock, to Mac's chagrin. Louis Riel shares with cowboy artist Charlie Russell the title of the worst Montana sheep herder, ever.[111]

After his brief sheepherding career, by late August 1882, Louis Riel was in Fort Benton, preparing to depart downriver by mackinaw to Carroll, at the mouth of the Musselshell River. Carroll had been started in the mid-1870s as an alternative port to Fort Benton. After a few prosperous years with Coulson Line steamboats, Carroll faded into history.[112] By the early 1880s, Carroll had become a small settlement of Métis occupying the surviving log cabins.

Riel had become acquainted with Fort Benton commission merchant T.C. Power and Power's agent at Carroll, Thomas O'Hanlon. The Métis at Carroll and other settlements in the rough Upper Missouri River country hunted the last of the bison. Their settlements were targeted by whiskey traders, and alcohol was rampant. Riel procured trade goods from O'Hanlon, likely on credit, and traded with the Métis and Native Indian hunters in exchange for buffalo robes. This afforded the Riels a meagre living, and it enabled Louis to engage in his complex mission—remaining close to his people, suppressing the whiskey trade and building bridges with Republican Party leaders in Montana.

Before departing Fort Benton, in September, Riel met Alexander C. Botkin, who was campaigning to defeat Democrat Martin Maginnis as Montana's territorial delegate in Congress. Marshal Botkin described their meeting:

In September 1882, while I was making a canvas of Montana in the effort to convince the people that they needed my service in congress, I visited Fort Benton. While I was there a figure appeared in my room that was quite sufficient to fix my attention and excite my interest. It was that of a man of magnificent stature, six feet in height, with broad shoulders, slightly rounded, and finely proportioned throughout. He had brown hair reaching to the neck, and a full beard of the same color. His complexion was that of a Caucasian, and there was nothing in his appearance save prominent cheek bones to suggest Indian blood. There was a notable dignity in his carriage, and he had a courtliness of manner that we are in the habit of regarding as characteristic of the French.

My interest in my caller was increased when he gave his name. I had read of the uprising of the Métis at Winnipeg in 1870 and was not a little impressed to find myself in the presence of the ex-president of the Republic of Manitoba, Louis Riel.

Addressing me in correct English, which he pronounced with a slight French accent, he made known the purpose of his call. This was to secure my official aid (I was then United States marshal) in prosecuting traders who were selling liquor to half-breeds. As I had not at that time been educated up to the practice that may be called the elastic enforcement of the laws—the custom of punishing some offenders and protecting others in a monopoly of law breaking—I encouraged him to procure the necessary evidence and promised my co-operation. After my return home I received several letters from him written with admirable precision in a hand that was almost feminine in its fineness. Nothing came of this, for the reason, among others, that the half-breeds were not Indians in charge of an agent or superintendent, and that the sale of liquor to them was scarcely within the purview of the laws of the United States. However, the incident possibly possesses some significance as showing the care that Riel exhibited in guarding the welfare of his people. He was himself a man of exemplary habits and intensely religious.[113]

Becoming heavily involved in Montana politics, Riel sought to deliver the Métis vote to Botkin, the Republican candidate for territorial delegate to Congress. In a letter to Delegate Maginnis of October 16, Riel wrote powerfully that he would not vote for Democrats for several reasons, including the following:

First. Up to the present time the Democratic press of the territory seem to have never thought that they had any justice or fairness to observe regarding American half-breed citizens.

Second. The contempt for their interests is so general among the Democrats of the Territory that even the officials of the county have taken advantage of it, year after year, to pillage them in the most open and scandalous manner.

[And concluding:] As to Mr. Botkin, I think that he is disposed and willing to protect the best interests of every American citizen, regardless of race or color, and, therefore, I have offered him my support, and he shall have it.[114]

In the election in the fall of 1882, Riel delivered the Métis votes even though he was not yet an American citizen, nor were his Métis followers. Riel was arrested by Choteau County sheriff John J. Healy, a fervent Democrat. A grand jury, under foreman and mayor of Fort Benton Jere Sullivan, indicted Riel for infringement of the election laws. After the court proceedings had dragged on for six months, thanks to the skill of his defense attorney, local Republican leader Herbert P. Rolfe, the charges were dismissed.[115]

St. Peter's Church today, where Louis Riel taught at the Indian Boys School before returning to Canada to lead his people. *Author's photo.*

On March 16, 1883, Louis Riel became an American citizen, and he was appointed deputy U.S. marshal in his efforts to suppress the whiskey trade. Meanwhile, he sought to improve his finances and family life by moving to St. Peter's Mission, where he was hired by the Jesuits to teach at their new boys' school. Riel apparently liked his new occupation teaching Native, Métis and White boys, and his performance was well received by the Jesuits, their only criticism being that he was too interested in politics. In September, the Riels welcomed their second daughter, Marie Angelique, at the mission.

On June 4, 1884, Riel was attending mass in St Peter's Mission when he was summoned to meet visitors. He found four Métis leaders, Gabriel Dumont, Moise Ouellette, Michel Dumas and James Isbister, who had come five hundred miles from the Métis settlements in northern Saskatchewan on a mission to recruit Riel to lead them in a campaign to redress grievances against Canada. Riel accepted on June 5. The die was cast.[116]

THE RED RIVER REBELLION

Returning to Canada, Riel held a series of meetings in which, at first, his tone was pacific but gradually became more violent, as his views turned from loyal agitation to rebellion. *Harper's Weekly* noted at the time,

> [Riel] *is a man of strong natural parts…and is imbued with a sense of what he believes* [are] *the wrongs suffered by the Half-breeds.…His past career shows him to be capable of leadership, and full of determination, and his suppression threatens to be no easy task.*[117]

The rebellion followed, and in its aftermath, Riel was tried and hanged. In the changing times of today, Louis Riel has become a Canadian national hero.[118]

Montana shares a colorful heritage with the Canadian West—and Louis Riel's exile years in Montana, centered on Fort Benton, are a heroic tribute. In the words of Regina, Manitoba scholar Dr. B.G. Dobbs, Louis Riel was far from being a bloody revolutionary but rather "a saintly idealist, a 19th century forerunner of Gandhi."[119]

With the failure of the rebellion, Riel was tried and convicted by Canadian authorities. *Author's collection.*

Dobbs has worked with Riel's diaries that chronicle the North-West Rebellion of 1885 and his prison days before his hanging in Regina for high treason. He believes the diaries are, "in a special sense, the birth certificate of the Canadian North-West.…And at the same time these diaries are also the death warrant of the once-proud Métis Nation."[120]

Dobbs writes,

> *Louis Riel, the tragic victor of the Red River Rebellion, the president of the provisional government of Manitoba, the founder of that province and the leader of the Métis National Committee was unable to repeat the victory of 1870.*
>
> *The opening of the Canadian west to settlers, the coming of the railway and the virtual extinction of the buffalo herds all meant an end to the way of life which the Métis had led on the Canadian Plains for centuries.*[121]

Chapter 14

A MULTICULTURAL MELTING POT

Fort Benton

From the 1831 founding of Fort Piegan at the mouth of the Marias on the Upper Missouri River, the absence of White women led to a long tradition of trader unions with Native women. These biracial unions contributed valuable ties between the series of trading posts and the Native Nations. The Fort Benton Trading Post began operations in 1846–47 with an average of about fifty traders and workers resident there, many with Native wives, principally from Blackfoot tribes. The factor (head trader) Alexander Culbertson; his Kainai wife, Natoyist-Siksina, daughter of Chief Two Suns; and their métis children exemplified these practical and politically astute unions.

From the dawn of the fur trade on the Upper Missouri, African Americans in modest numbers—a few slaves, most free men—were present. During the winter of 1862–63, the residents of Fort Benton Trading Post numbered thirty-seven men. Many of these men were French Canadians, who had a long tradition of life as trappers and traders. Notably, three Blacks were present—Henry Mills, Philip Barnes and James Vanlitburg—and no White women. The presence and names of Native women and métis children were not recorded in this survey.

From 1863 onward, as the community of Fort Benton began to grow adjacent to the trading post, the town's residents formed a truly multicultural society with biracial White-Native and Black-Native families and foreign-born Whites, later joined by Chinese.

Fort Benton adventurers. *Standing, left to right:* Jewish Mose Solomon, African American Bob Mills and John Largent. *Seated, left to right:* Métis Joe Kipp and Henry Kennerly. *OHRC.*

Complicating the environment throughout Montana Territory, created in 1864 during the Civil War, was the rush into Montana's gold mining camps by thousands of southern and border state secessionists and Confederates. The far distant land of the Upper Missouri became the exile of choice for many southern men and their families fleeing the violence of their war-torn homes. Other southerners came to honor paroles banishing them to the "western territories" or because their Confederate units were losing the war

Three Blackfeet wives of traders with children posed in Dan Dutro's photographic studio in Fort Benton in the 1880s. *Author's collection.*

in the western theater of Missouri and Tennessee—bringing an element of truth to the Montana legend that the "left wing of Price's Army" came to Montana Territory.[122]

Early Fort Benton featured a multiracial melting pot bordering on a power keg, and—perhaps without oversimplification—early Fort Benton society formed a hierarchy with Whites at the top, followed roughly in order of apparent acceptance by White-Blacks, Black Americans, White-Native métis children, Chinese and, at the bottom, male Natives, few of whom dared to reside in the town. Among the Whites, too, there was a diverse mix of the old resident fur traders and a new influx of southerners from the border states and immigrant Irish, many having served in Union army Irish brigades—in fact, a strong Irish Fenian element gained power by 1870 through alliance with Southern Democrats. An important final element in early Fort Benton was the presence of a U.S. Army infantry company from the regiment stationed nearby in Fort Shaw—for most of the 1870s, this would be the 7th U.S. Infantry. From 1869 to 1881, army officers, some with wives, and soldiers were present—many foreign-born—and a major influence in security and social affairs.

The many Native wives of White men formed a special category, numerous and accepted until greater numbers of White women began to arrive from the late 1870s until the end of the nineteenth century. In addition, at least four White-Black marriages and the occasional Black-Native family further complicated Fort Benton's racial diversity.

A close examination of the June 1870 Fort Benton U.S. Census reflects the multicultural town. Among the 435 residents of Fort Benton in 1870 were 47 White-Native families and 1 Black-Native family. Black Henry Mills, who long worked at the trading post, was recorded in 1870 as a sixty-two-year-old laborer, born in Kentucky, with his thirty-seven-year-old Native wife, Phillisy, and their seventeen-year-old biracial daughter, Mary.

Overall, by 1870, the town, fueled by the active steamboat trade, had become a major center of commerce and was growing from its beginning in 1863, with 160 dwellings, 210 White males and just 6 White females—one, Nellie Montgomery, age twenty-seven, was apparently unmarried. Five White children were present: Clevenger Eastman, four, with his merchant father, F.H. Eastman, forty, and his mother, Sarah E., twenty-eight; Katy, two months old, with her mother, Katy, twenty-eight, whose husband, S.J. Perkins, thirty-two, was a prosperous auctioneer; Charles B., age three, with his mother Mary G., twenty-five, whose husband, Tom C. Power, was becoming one of the town's "merchant princes"; and Louisa, age eight, and John, six, with their mother Margaret, thirty-two, whose husband, Winfield Scott Stocking, thirty-three, was a prosperous butcher.[123]

BLACK RESIDENTS IN 1870

Reflecting the prosperity of the town, Fort Benton had nineteen African Americans, fifteen Black males and four Black females:

Julia Davis, twenty-five, born in Missouri, domestic servant in the household of White First Lieutenant William B. Pease, Blackfeet Indian agent.

Maria Berry, thirty-eight, from Tennessee, domestic servant in the household of White M.A. Flanagan; M. Dennis, twenty-five, Missouri, cook; and John Kelly, twenty-five, Missouri, laborer in the Flanagan household.

Emma Morris, thirty-two, Virginia, house servant in the household of F.H. Eastman.

Young Ed Simms served as clerk on the steamboat *Red Cloud* and, on arrival at Fort Benton, decided to remain on the Upper Missouri, working for Fort Shaw post trader McKnight before settling as the first Black resident in the new town of Great Falls. *Author's collection.*

John Davis, twenty-nine, Missouri, laborer and head of household, with Sol Warrick, fifty-two, Virginia, barber, and George Johnson, thirty-one, Missouri, servant.

William B. Hawkins, thirty, Missouri, cook in the household of White laborer Charles Hardy.

Henry Mills, sixty-two, Kentucky, laborer, with Native wife Phillisy, thirty-seven, and their daughter Mary, seventeen and a half, Native.

John Hughes, thirty-three, Kentucky, teamster, in the household of White teamster Louis F. Carson.

Leamer Davis, forty, Louisiana, domestic servant and head of his own household.

John Ross, thirty-six, mulatto, South Carolina, barber and head of household with Alex Clark, twenty-one, mulatto, Missouri, barber, and Richard Lamb, twenty-seven, mulatto, Indiana, barber.

James Vanlitburg, fifty-five, Virginia, domestic servant and head of household with David H. Dolbec, sixty-two, Louisiana, domestic servant.

John Walker, fifty-two, Missouri, servant in the Overland Hotel, operated by White Robert Mills.[124]

CHINESE RESIDENTS IN 1870

The 1870 census recorded three Chinese living in Fort Benton, all born in China and working as washermen in a Chinese laundry: Hao Chang, forty; Wong Lee, twenty-eight; and Loy Sam, thirty-two.[125]

Chinese laundryman walking in Fort Benton's Chinese Garden. *OHRC.*

MILITARY POST FORT BENTON

From 1869 through 1881, Fort Benton Military Post was garrisoned by one company from the army regiment at Fort Shaw, located sixty miles to the west. On June 13, 1870, Company E of the 7th Infantry, commanded by Major William B. Lewis, relieved the 13th Infantry at Fort Benton, just six weeks before the 1870 U.S. Census was conducted on August 2. The garrison consisted of fifty-nine men and five women and one baby girl—all White, with a majority foreign-born, thirty-two men and four women. The following women were in the garrison:

Rebecca, age twenty-four, born in Florida, with her husband, R. Abraham, thirty-eight, born in Ireland, a soldier, and Anne Hoban, twenty-two, born in Ireland, with her husband, Thomas Hoban, thirty-three, born in Ireland, a soldier. Both Rebecca and Anne served as laundresses.

Mary, twenty-four, born in England, with her daughter, Mary, age one, born in Utah, and her husband, Samuel Bellow, twenty-nine, born in New York, a soldier.

Anna, twenty-seven, born in Ireland, a laundress, with her husband, Mitchel Fallon, forty-two, born in Ireland, a soldier.

Mary, thirty, born in Ireland, a laundress, with her husband, Pat Fallon, twenty-six, born in Ireland, a soldier.[126]

THE BEAR RIVER MASSACRE

January 23, 1870, indelibly marks one of the most tragic events in Montana history—the Marias Massacre, known by the Blackfoot as the Bear River Massacre. On that bitterly cold early winter morning, four troops of 2nd Cavalry from Fort Ellis, under the command of Major Eugene Baker, joined by fifty-five men of the Mounted Detachment 13th Infantry from Fort Shaw, attacked the smallpox-ravaged, sleeping camp of Piegan chief Heavy Runner, killing about two hundred people. The murdered included Heavy Runner, who tried to stop the carnage. Many other victims of the attack were sick with smallpox—most were women, children and the elderly. Many adult men were away hunting buffalo.[127]

Among the later testimonies, young survivor Bear Head emotionally recounted:

> (A)t once all the seizers [soldiers] *began shooting into the lodges. Chief Heavy Runner ran from his lodge toward the seizers on the (river) bank. He*

was shouting to them and waving a paper...a writing saying that he was a good and peaceful man, a friend of the whites. He had run but a few steps when he fell, his body pierced with bullets.

Inside the lodges men were yelling, terribly frightened women and children screaming, screaming from wounds, from pain as they died. I saw a few men and women escaping from the lodges, shot down as they ran....I sat before the ruin of my lodge and felt sick. I wished the seizers had killed me, too.[128]

Following the brutal massacre, the soldiers burned the tipis and other possessions and rounded up the Native horses, decreasing the likelihood that those who survived the attack would be able to survive the harsh winter conditions. Initially, the Montana press hailed Baker as a hero, but gradually, reports by both Natives and non-Natives questioned his version of events, exposing the true atrocities that took place on the Marias River.

In the mind of Harvard-educated Blackfeet scholar Darryl Kipp, the massacre stands as one of three great blows to the Blackfeet Nation. The

Marias River site of the massacre of Heavy Runner's camp of Blackfeet in January 1870. Photo likely by A.B. Coe. *OHRC.*

first terrible blow was in 1837, when three-fifths of the tribe perished in a smallpox epidemic brought on by contaminated trade goods. Kipp believes "the massacre probably was the ultimate crushing blow. It was something they never really recovered from. Previously, they would have fought back. They were unable to. They had to accept the massacre. The massacre was an extremely violent blow to the spirit of the people."[129]

To Kipp, the final great blow came in 1884, when the buffalo were totally gone from the plains, leaving the Blackfeet destitute in that "starvation winter."[130]

The Massacre Survivors

In the aftermath of the massacre, Blackfeet Indian agent Lieutenant William A. Pease was directed to gather facts and testimony about the survivors. Pease reported 173 Blackfeet killed: 33 men (15 aged twelve to thirty-seven and 18 aged thirty-seven to seventy), 90 women (35 aged twelve to thirty-seven and 55 aged thirty-seven to seventy) and 50 children (younger than twelve years, including many babies). Yet Joe Kipp determined there were 217 victims.

Pease recorded a total of fifty-one survivors: eighteen women, nineteen small children and infants, nine young men and five hunters away from camp.[131]

This author has identified a total of twenty-eight survivors of the Bear Creek Massacre, and they are listed below. Among these twenty-eight, nine may be women, eleven children, seven young men and one hunter. Some survivors of the attack likely died of wounds, while others froze to death. The survivors may have made their way to other Piegan camps along the river. Yet legend has it that some of the survivors made their way down the Marias River to Fort Benton, desperately seeking refuge and assistance from the large community of Native women then living in the town—at least seventy-four Native women likely were present in Fort Benton at the time.

The following Bear River Massacre survivor list presents those from Heavy Runner's camp, including Wolf Eagle, who may have been one of the hunters.

Almost A Dog (Imazí-imita): Wounded but survived. Adult man.
Bear Head (Kai Otokan): age fourteen; was tending horse herd. Heavy Runner's nephew.
Black Antelope: Wounded but survived. Old man.

Black Eagle: Wounded but survived. Adult man.

Buffalo Trail Woman: Age twenty-two in January 1870. Husband Good Stab/Yellow Owl was killed.

Catches Inside: Mother of Mary Middle Calf. Mrs. Frank Monroe's mother.

Charging at Night: Heavy Runner's wife, Spear Woman's mother.

Comes With Tattles, or William Heavy Runner Kipp Upham: Cousin of Bear Head.

Curlew Woman: Age forty-one.

Double Strike Woman: Age ten. Older sister of Spear Woman. First wife of Joseph Kipp.

First Kill Margaret: Spanish, daughter of Curlew Woman.

Fog Eater: Wounded but survived. Adult man.

Good Bear Woman: Married No Chief, Piegan.

Heard-by-Both Sides Woman

Heavy Runner Baby: Died shortly after.

Holy Bear Woman/Holy Medicine Bear Woman Pace (Natohkyiaakii): Married Frederick Pace.

Last Gun, Dick Heavy Runner Kipp: Age seven or fourteen. Son of Heavy Runner.

Long Time Calf: Eight years old.

Martha Heavy Runner Gobert Kennerly Kipp: Daughter of Heavy Runner.

Mary Middle Calf: Daughter of Catches Inside.

Red Paint Woman: Shot in the leg but survived.

Spear Woman (Sapapistatsaki) or Emma Heavy Runner Upham Miller: Age six. Daughter of Heavy Runner.

Susan Heavy Runner Fitzpatrick: Daughter of Heavy Runner.

Spopee (Turtle): Kainai.

Takes Gun at Night, "Cut Bank John," Heavy Runner Kipp: Age ten. Son of Heavy Runner, raised by Joe Kipp.

Three Bears: Old man.

Wolf Eagle: A hunter.

Wolf Leader[132]

NOTES

Introduction

1. Among the best sources for Fort Benton's history are Lepley, *Birthplace of Montana*; Lepley, *Blackfoot Fur Trade*; Lepley, *Packets to Paradise*; Overholser, *Fort Benton*; Robison, "Completing the Mullan Road"; Robison, *Historical Fort Benton*; Robison, *Whoop-Up Country*; Robison, *Yankees and Rebels*.
2. The "Medicine Line" is the United States–Canada border along the forty-ninth parallel in the west. Natives called this border the Medicine Line because during the Frontier Wars, American troops respected it as if by magic.
3. Overholser, *Fort Benton*, 225.
4. Gladstone, "Views of Early Fort Benton," *Rocky Mountain Echo*, December 8, 1903.

Chapter 1

5. *Flathead Courier*, June 19, 1919. For saving the historic Fort Benton Blockhouse, see www.kenrobisonhistory.com/fort-benton-tales.
6. *Great Falls Tribune*, December 15, 1929.

Chapter 2

7. James H. Bradley military records, Fold3.
8. *Contributions to the Historical Society of Montana*, vol. 2; Bradley, *Montana Column*.
9. *Benton Record*, August 17, 1877.
10. *Helena Herald*, August 16, 1877.
11. *Benton Record*, June 29, 1877; *Contributions to MHS*, vols. 1, 2, 3, 8 and 9.
12. The *Benton Record* published Lieutenant Bradley's articles under his nom de plume, "Cavalier."
13. *Benton Record*, February 15, 1875; Major Alexander Culbertson named his trading post for Senator Thomas H. Benton of St. Louis for his services to the American Fur Company.

Chapter 3

14. *Montana Post*, June 3, 1865.
15. *Bozeman Courier*, December 16, 1927; Robison, "Robison-Wahlberg List."
16. Robison, "Robison-Wahlberg List."
17. *Big Sandy Mountaineer*, February 17, 1927.
18. Ibid.
19. *Sioux City Register*, June 17, 1865; Chittenden, *Early Steamboat Navigation* vol. 2, 279; *Montana Post*, July 8, 1865.
20. Healy, *Life and Death*, 166–69.
21. Blackfoot Kainai killed Joe Spearman at Fort Whoop-Up on the Belly River in 1870. Bostwick served as a scout with Colonel John Gibbons's 7th Infantry; he was killed at the Battle of the Big Hole on August 9, 1877.
22. The men with Sheriff Neil Howie were Captain Frank Moore, commanding *Cutter*; John H. Rogers, politician; Captain Nick Wall, manager of John J. Roe's Diamond R. Freighting and retail store; and Malcolm Clark, rancher and fur trader. *Montana Post*, July 8, 1865.
23. *Sioux City Register*, June 17, 1865.
24. Matthew Carroll & George Steell, formerly American Fur Company, partners in Fort Benton store; *Montana Post*, July 8, 1865.
25. *Montana Post*, June 10, 1865.

Chapter 4

26. Hamilton died in Stillwater County in 1908, age eighty-five. He left St. Louis in 1842 with a company of free trappers under Bill Williams. Hamilton wrote about many of his early adventures, compiled in Silliman, *We Seized Our Rifles*.
27. *River Press*, April 19, 1961.
28. Under the 1865 treaty, the Blackfeet agreed to sell two thousand square miles of the territory south of the Missouri River. This treaty was never ratified by Congress, yet settlers moved in anyway. *Big Timber Pioneer*, January 19, 1920.
29. *River Press*, December 24, 1884; Overholser, *Fort Benton*, 380.

Chapter 5

30. *St. Louis Post Dispatch*, June 18, 1943.
31. *River Press*, June 21, 1989.
32. Towle, *Vigilante Woman*, 88–103.
33. *St. Louis Post-Dispatch*, June 6, 1943.
34. "Old Man River—Famous Woman Gambler," *St. Louis Post-Dispatch*, June 18, 1943. For more about Madame Dumont's death and virtues, see www.kenrobisonhistory.com/fort-benton-tales.

Chapter 6

35. Lieutenant James Bradley, writing as "Cavalier," recorded the story of Little Dog's lost treasure—see www.kenrobisonhistory.com/fort-benton-tales.
36. *River Press*, September 23, 1981; see www.kenrobisonhistory.com/fort-benton-tales for articles on Little Dog, the Mullan Road, the Experimental Farm and the Sun River Stampede.
37. Healy, *Life and Death*, 141–43.
38. *Montana Post*, June 9, 1866.

Chapter 7

39. Paul Wylie's *The Irish General Thomas Francis Meagher* provides the best biography of Meagher's Montana years; *Montana Post*, June 29, 1867.

40. "General Thomas Francis Meagher: The Fort Benton Mystery and Legend," *River Press*, June 24, 2009.

41. "Jury Concludes Meagher Was Murdered," *River Press*, July 1, 2009.

42. Montana Historical Society, Eugene Tucker Papers, SC2551, Tucker Letter Dated August 8, 1867.

43. *Anaconda Standard*, July 6, 1913.

44. *Montana Post*, July 13, 1867.

45. *Virginia Tri-Weekly Post*, July 9, 1867.

46. *Virginia Tri-Weekly Post*, July 9, 1867.

47. *Montana Post*, July 13, 1867.

48. *Virginia Tri-Weekly Post*, July 11, 1867.

49. *River Press*, June 24, 2009; *Montana Post*, June 29 and July 6, 13 and 20, 1867; *Helena Herald Weekly*, July 3 and 10, 1867; *Rocky Mountain Gazette*, July 6, 1867; Robison, "Robison-Wahlberg List."

Chapter 8

50. "Mrs. Thomas Francis Meagher's Sad Departure from Fort Benton in 1867: What a Way to Treat a Lady!" *River Press*, August 3, 2005.

51. Athearn, *Irish Revolutionary*, 166–67.

52. Forney, *Irish Rebel*, 218–19.

53. *Montana Post*, July 27, 1867.

54. *Montana Post*, August 17, 1867.

55. *Montana Post*, August 31, 1867.

56. *Montana Post*, November 9, 1867.

57. *Montana Post*, September 28, October 9, 1867; *Helena Herald*, September 5, 1867; Robison, "Robison-Wahlberg List."

Chapter 9

58. Commissioner of Indian Affairs, "No. 77½ Correspondence."

59. *Montana Post*, June 9, 1866.

60. Hanson, *Grant Marsh*, 76–77.

61. *River Press*, March 21, 1984.
62. Culbertson, *Joseph Culbertson*, 2–3.
63. *Montana Post*, August 28, 1868. In May 1867, Colonel George W. Hynson assumed command of the newly raised First Regiment, Montana Militia. *Montana Post*, May 18, 1867.
64. *Montana Post*, August 28, 1868.
65. "Murderer Who Was Marshal of Fort Benton Dug Own Grave and Bought the Rope With Which Vigilantes Hanged Him," *Conrad Independent*, November 28, 1918.
66. Langford, *Vigilante Days*, 330–332.
67. "Murderer Who Was Marshal."
68. *River Press*, May 8, 1901.
69. "Murderer Who Was Marshal."
70. Langford, *Vigilante Days*, 335.
71. Lowell, *Lost Memoir*, 106–11.
72. *River Press*, March 21, 1984, "Vigilante Vengeance for Bowlegs"; *Helena Herald*, April 7, 1871.
73. Lowell, *Lost Memoir*, 106–8.
74. Ibid., 111.
75. *Helena Herald*, February 15, 1872.
76. Ibid.
77. *Helena Weekly Herald*, November 19, 1868.
78. *Dillon Examiner*, December 17, 1941.
79. *Helena Weekly Herald*, December 5, 1872.
80. Lepley, *Birthplace*, 53–55.

Chapter 10

81. *Great Falls Tribune*, April 5, 1903; X. Beidler is interred in Forestvale Cemetery, Helena.
82. "M'Cormick Saw Scalping of 173 Helpless Indians," *Dillon Examiner*, December 17, 1941.
83. Overholser, *Fort Benton*, 55–56.
84. "'X': A Frequent Benton Visitor," *River Press*, June 4, 1986.
85. *Montana Post*, June 29, 1867.
86. "Al H. Wilkins Tells of Experiences in Montana in Early Seventies," *Great Falls Tribune*, July 1, 1934.
87. *Benton Record*, June 26, 1875.
88. *Benton Record*, February 26, 1876.

89. *Benton Record*, April 15, 1876.

90. Robison, "Robison-Wahlberg List."

91. Farr, *Blackfoot Redemption*, 62–64; Spopee's compelling story is told by Dr. William E. Farr in *Blackfoot Redemption*.

Chapter 11

92. *Benton Record*, November 9, 1882; Murphy, *Half Interest*, 112.

93. *River Press*, October 11, 1882.

94. *Benton Record*, November 9, 1882.

95. "Grand Union Hotel's 140th Anniversary: Nov. 2, 1882–Nov. 2, 2022," *River Press*, November 2, 2022.

96. Ibid.

97. Ibid.

Chapter 12

98. Vivian, *Treasures for America*, 14–16.

99. *River Press*, July 26, 1882.

100. *Bismarck Tribune*, July 21, 1882.

101. "January 19 1883—First Time Use Of Electric Lighting System," Maps of World, www.mapsofworld.com/on-this-day/january-19-1883-overhead-wires-are-used-for-an-electric-lighting-system-for-the-first-time-designed-by-thomas-edison-for-roselle-new-jersey/.

102. Murphy, *Half Interest*, 112.

Chapter 13

103. "Louis Riel, Leader of Indian and French Canadian Half-Breeds in Famous Riel Rebellion Once Lived in Montana," *Conrad Independent*, February 5, 1925.

104. Payment, *Riel Family*, 84.

105. *Benton Record*, December 19, 1879.

106. Naturalization papers missing from clerk of court, Chouteau County Courthouse. Dated May 17, 1880, book 1, page 67; likely burned in 1882 courthouse fire, "Louis Riel" Vertical File, Overholser Historical Research Center.

107. Martel, *Collected Works of Louis Riel*, vol. 2, 223–26.
108. *Benton Record*, September 17, 1880.
109. Thomas, "Riel, Louis"; Wikipedia, "Louis Riel."
110. Banks, *Wandersong*, 255–57.
111. Ibid.
112. Lepley, *Packets to Paradise*, 159–60.
113. *Great Falls Tribune*, September 9, 1900.
114. *Helena Herald*, October 20, 1882.
115. *Benton Record*, August 24, 1883; *River Press*, April 23, 1884.
116. *Sun River Sun*, June 12, 1884; *River Press*, June 18, 1884.
117. *Conrad Independent*, February 2, 1925.
118. For more about Riel's role in the 1885 Red River Rebellion, see www.kenrobisonhistory.com/fort-benton-tales.
119. *Star-Phoenix* (Saskatoon, SK), May 26, 1971.
120. Ibid.
121. Ibid.

Chapter 14

122. Robison's *Yankees and Rebels* and *Confederates* explore the influx of southerners into Montana Territory during and after the Civil War.
123. See www.kenrobisonhistory.com/fort-benton-tales for a complete listing for Fort Benton residents in the 1870 U.S. Census.
124. For tales of African Americans in Fort Benton, see Robison, *Yankees and Rebels*, 127–73.
125. For tales of Chinese in Fort Benton, see www.kenrobisonhistory.com/fort-benton-tales.
126. For listing of the garrison at Fort Benton Military Post in 1870, see www.kenrobisonhistory.com/fort-benton-tales.
127. Wylie, *Blood on the Marias*, 181–201.
128. *Bozeman Chronicle*, January 25, 2012.
129. Ibid.
130. Ibid.
131. Henderson, *Marias Massacre*, 62.
132. Some estimates of casualties are as high as 225. See www.kenrobisonhistory.com/fort-benton-tales for biographies of Bear River survivors. Additions and corrections to this list with documentation are welcomed—send via author website www.kenrobisonhistory.com.

BIBLIOGRAPHY

Online Resources

Fold3 Military Records. https://www.fold3.com.

Gibson, Stan, and Jack Hayne. "Witnesses to Carnage: The 1870 Marias Massacre in Montana." First Nation Issues of Consequence. Accessed February 15, 2023. www.dickshovel.com/parts2.html.

Julien, Henry. "Six Months in the Wilds of the North-West." *Canadian Illustrated News.* www.canadiana.ca/view/oocihm.8_06230.

Legends of America. "James Berry—A Little Known Outlaw from Missouri." Accessed February 14, 2023. www.legendsofamerica.com/we-jamesberry.html.

Maps of World. "January 19 1883—First Time Use of Electric Lighting System." Accessed February 15, 2023. www.mapsofworld.com/on-this-day/january-19-1883-overhead-wires-are-used-for-an-electric-lighting-system-for-the-first-time-designed-by-thomas-edison-for-roselle-new-jersey/.

Robison, Ken. "Tales of Fort Benton." www.kenrobisonhistory.com/fort-benton-tales.

———. *Historical Fort Benton* (blog). http://fortbenton.blogspot.com/.

Thomas, Lewis H. "Riel, Louis (1844–85)." *Dictionary of Canadian Biography.* http://www.biographi.ca/en/bio/riel_louis_1844_85_11E.html.

Wikipedia. "Louis Riel." https://en.wikipedia.org/wiki/Louis_Riel. Accessed February 15, 2023.

Newspapers & Journals (Montana Unless Otherwise Noted)

Benton Weekly Record
Big Sandy Mountaineer
Big Timber Pioneer
Billings Gazette
Bismarck Tribune (North Dakota)
Bozeman Chronicle
Bozeman Courier
Calgary Herald (Canada)
Canadian Illustrated News (Canada)
Conrad Independent
Dillon Examiner
Fort Benton River Press
Great Falls Tribune
Helena Independent
Helena Weekly Herald
Montana Post (Virginia City)
Montana Radiator (Helena)
New-North-West (Deer Lodge)
Rocky Mountain Echo (Pincher Creek, Alberta, Canada)
Rocky Mountain Gazette (Helena)
Sioux City (Iowa) Register
Star-Phoenix (Saskatoon, Saskatchewan, Canada)
St. Louis (Missouri) Post-Dispatch
Sun River Sun

Books and Other Sources

Arthur, Jim, ed. *Retracing Kipp Family Trails: A Collection of Stories and Pictures of the Kipp Family and the Country They Lived In, with Stories by Octavia Kipp.* Lewistown, MT: Central Montana, 1997.

Athearn, Robert G. *Thomas Francis Meagher: An Irish Revolutionary in America.* Boulder: University of Colorado Press, 1949.

Banks, Eleanor. *Wandersong.* Caldwell, ID: Caxton, 1950.

Baumler, Ellen. *Beyond Spirit Tailings: Montana's Mysteries, Ghosts and Haunted Places.* Helena, MT: Historical Society Press, 2005.

Blackfeet Heritage Program. *Blackfeet Heritage, 1907–1908.* Browning, MT: Blackfeet Heritage Program, 1980.

Bradley, Lieutenant James H. *The March of the Montana Column: A Prelude to the Custer Disaster.* Edited by Edgar I. Steward. Norman: University of Oklahoma Press, 1961.

Chittenden, Hiram Martin. *History of Early Steamboat Navigation on the Missouri River: Life and Adventures of Joseph La Barge.* 2 vols. New York: Francis P. Harper, 1903.

Contributions to the Historical Society of Montana. Vols. 1, 2, 3, 8 & 9. Helena: various publishers, 1876–1910.

Culbertson, Joseph. *Joseph Culbertson: Famous Indian Scout Who Served under General Miles in 1876–1895 True Stories of Camp Life in the Early Days.* Wolf Point, MT: Frank Delger, 1958.

Dempsey, Hugh A. *The Amazing Death of Calf Shirt and Other Blackfoot Stories: Three Hundred Years of Blackfoot History.* Norman: University of Oklahoma Press, 1994.

———. *Firewater: The Impact of the Whisky Trade on the Blackfoot Nation.* Calgary: Fifth House, 2002.

———. *Jerry Potts, Plainsman.* Occasional Paper No. 3. Calgary: Glenbow Foundation, 1966.

Denny, Sir Cecil. *Denny's Trek: A Mountie's Memoir of the March West.* Surrey, BC: Heritage House, 2004.

Donovan, Tom. *Hanging Around the Big Sky: The Unofficial Guide to Lynching, Strangling and Legal Hangings of Montana—Book Two: Extra-Legal Hangings.* Great Falls, MT: Portage Meadows, 2008.

Ege, Robert J. *Tell Baker to Strike Them Hard.* Bellevue, NE: Old Army Press, 1970.

Farr, William E. *Blackfoot Redemption: A Blood Indian's Story of Murder, Confinement, and Imperfect Justice.* Norman: University of Oklahoma Press, 2014.

Forney, Gary R. *Thomas Francis Meagher: Irish Rebel, American Yankee, Montana Pioneer.* Self-published, Xlibris, 2003.

The Frontier Art of R.B. Nevitt: Surgeon, North-West Mounted Police, 1874–78. Calgary: Glenbow-Alberta Institute, n.d.

Gladstone, William. "Views of Early Fort Benton." *Rocky Mountain Echo*, December 8, 1903.

Graybill, Andrew R. *The Red and the White: A Family Saga of the American West.* New York: Liveright, 2013.

Greene, Jerome A. *Nez Perce Summer 1877: The U. S. Army and the Nee-Me-Poo Crisis.* Helena: Montana Historical Society Press, 2000.

Hanson, Joseph Mills. *The Conquest of the Missouri: Being the Story of the Life and Exploits of Captain Grant Marsh*. New York: Murray Hill Books, 1909.

———. *When Skins Were Money: A History of the Fur Trade*. Chadron, NE: Museum of the Fur Trade, 2005.

Harris-Berry Family Material Collected by William H. Patterson. Held at Overholser Historical Research Center, Fort Benton.

Healy, John J. *Life and Death on the Upper Missouri: The Frontier Sketches of Johnny Healy*. Edited by Ken Robison. Self-published, Create Space Independent Publishing Platform, 2013.

Henderson, Rodger C. "The Piikuni and the U.S. Army's Piegan Expedition: Competing Narratives of the 1870 Massacre on the Marias River." *Montana: The Magazine of Western History* (Spring 2018): 48–96.

Kennedy, M.A., and B.O.K. Reeves. *An Inventory and Historical Description of Whiskey Posts in Southern Alberta*. Edmonton, Alberta: Historic Sites Service, Old St. Stephen's College, 1984.

Langford, Nathaniel Pitt. *Vigilante Days and Ways—The Pioneers of the Rockies— The Makers and Making of Montana, Idaho, Oregon, Washington, and Wyoming*. Boston, J.G. Cupples, 1890.

Lepley, John G. *Birthplace of Montana: A History of Fort Benton*. Missoula, MT: Pictorial Histories, 1999.

———. *Blackfoot Fur Trade on the Upper Missouri*. Missoula, MT: Pictorial Histories, 2004.

———. *The Madame and the Four Johns: Fort Benton's Lawless Years of Gold,* Fort Benton, MT: River & Plains Society, 2013.

———. *Packets to Paradise: Steamboating to Fort Benton*. Missoula, MT: Pictorial Histories, 2001.

Long, Philip S. *Jerry Potts: Scout, Frontiersman and Hero*. Calgary: Bonanza Books, 1974.

Lowell, James Howard. *An Antietam Veteran's Montana Journey: The Lost Memoir of James Howard Lowell*. Edited by Katherine Seaton Squires. Charleston, SC: The History Press, 2018.

Martel, Gilles. *The Collected Writings of Louis Riel*. Vol. 2. Edmonton: University of Alberta Press, 1985.

McBride, Sister Genevieve, OSV. *The Bird Tail*. New York: Vantage Press, 1974.

McDermott, Paul D., et al, eds. *The Mullan Road: Carving a Passage through the Frontier Northwest, 1859–62*. Missoula, MT: Mountain Press Publishing, 2015.

Montana Historical Society. SC2551 Folders 1 and 2, Eugene Tucker Papers.

Murphy, James E. *Half Interest in a Silver Dollar: The Saga of Charles E. Conrad.* Missoula, MT: Mountain Press, 1983.

Overholser, Joel. *Fort Benton: World's Innermost Port.* Helena, MT: Falcon Press, 1987.

Payment, Diane. *Riel Family: Home and Lifestyle at St-Vital, 1860–1910.* Parks Canada, May 1980.

Robison, Ken. "Completing the Mullan Road from Mullan Pass to Fort Benton: A Harbinger of Change," in *The Mullan Road: Carving a Passage through the Frontier Northwest, 1859 to 1862*, edited by Paul D. McDermott (Missoula, MT: Mountain Press Publishing, 2015), 131–51.

———. *Confederates in Montana Territory: In the Shadow of Price's Army.* Charleston, SC: The History Press, 2014.

———. *Historic Tales of Whoop-Up Country: On the Trail from Montana's Fort Benton to Canada's Fort Macleod.* Charleston, SC: The History Press, 2020.

———. *Montana Territory and the Civil War: A Frontier Forged on the Battlefield.* Charleston, SC: The History Press, 2013.

———. "The Robison-Wahlberg List of Upper Missouri Steamboat Passengers." Unpublished work, author's collection.

———. *Yankees and Rebels on the Upper Missouri: Steamboats, Gold and Peace.* Charleston, SC: The History Press, 2016.

Schultz, James Willard. *Friends of My Life as an Indian.* Boston: Houghton Mifflin, 1923.

———. *My Life as an Indian.* Boston: Houghton, Mifflin, 1907.

Silliman, Lee. *We Seized Our Rifles.* Missoula: Mountain Press, 1982.

Strachan, John. *Blazing the Mullan Trail: Connecting the Headwaters of the Missouri and Columbia Rivers.* New York: Edward Eberstadt & Sons, 1952.

Tolton, Gordon E. *Healy's West: The Life and Times of John J. Healy.* Calgary: Heritage House, 2014.

Touchie, Rodger D. *Bear Child: The Life and Times of Jerry Potts.* Surrey, AB: Heritage House, 2005.

Towle, Virginia Rowe. *Vigilante Woman.* New York: A.S. Barnes, 1966.

Upson, Charles, and Hiram D. Upham. "No. 77½,—Correspondence showing hostilities of Blackfeet (3 letters)." Washington, D.C.: United States Office of the Commissioner of Indian Affairs, 1866. http://digitalcollections.lib.washington.edu/digital/collection/lctext/id/2819.

Vivian, Cassandra. *Treasures for America: Steamboats from the Monongahela Boatyards.* www.academia.edu/30401453/Steamboats_on_the_Mon_6_MOUNTAIN_BOATS.

Wischmann, Lesley. *Frontier Diplomats: Alexander Culbertson and Natoyist-Siksina among the Blackfeet.* Spokane, WA: University of Oklahoma Press, 2000.

Wischmann, Lesley, and Andrew Erskine Dawson. *This Far-Off Wild Land: The Upper Missouri Letters of Andrew Dawson.* Norman, OK: Arthur H. Clark, 2013.

Wissler, Clark, and Alice Beck Kehoe. *Amskapi Pikuni: The Blackfoot People.* Albany: State University of New York Press, 2012.

Wylie, Paul R. *Blood on the Marias: The Baker Massacre.* Norman: University of Oklahoma Press, 2016.

———. *The Irish General Thomas Francis Meagher.* Norman: University of Oklahoma Press, 2007.

INDEX

Vaughan, Alfred 76
Vielleaux, Narcisse (Nelse) 58
vigilantes 11, 16, 20, 63, 64, 86,
    100, 102, 103, 104, 105, 107,
    108, 110, 111, 112, 113, 114,
    115, 118, 120
Virginia City 13, 14, 36, 39, 40, 46,
    63, 82, 83, 93, 94, 95, 96, 103,
    105, 106, 135

W

wagon train 48, 84
Wall, Nick 42, 44, 46, 47
Weatherwax, John D. 19, 101
Wetzel, Winfield Scott 20, 137
Whites 12, 16, 40, 41, 44, 45, 54,
    55, 56, 57, 74, 76, 77, 79, 102,
    158, 160, 165
Whoop-Up Country 14, 18, 100,
    105, 108, 114, 120
Whoop-Up Trail 19, 22
Wilkins, Al 122, 123
Woods, James M. 42, 84, 87
Wylie, Paul 82, 86
Wypert, Pipeneaux 111, 112, 114

ABOUT THE AUTHOR

Ken Robison is a native Montanan and a chronicler of neglected western history. He is a trustee on the board of the Montana Historical Society and has been honored as a Montana Heritage Keeper. He is the historian at the Overholser Historical Research Center and for the Great Falls/Cascade County Historic Preservation Commission and is active in historic preservation throughout Montana. Ken is a retired captain after a career in naval intelligence. His most recent books include *Historic Tales of Whoop-Up Country: On the Trail from Montana's Fort Benton to Canada's Fort Macleod* and *Cold War Montana: From Stolen Secrets to the Ace in the Hole*. Visit his website, Ken Robison History, at https://www.kenrobisonhistory.com.

Author delivering the 175th anniversary tribute to Fort Benton during the annual summer celebration in 2021 at Old Fort Park. *Author's collection.*